GOT
YOUR
LEGENDS

ALSO BY MIKE GREENBERG AND HEMBO

Got Your Number
Got Your Answers

GOT
YOUR
LEGENDS

RANKING AMERICA'S
SPORTS FRANCHISES AND THEIR
MOST ICONIC FIGURES

MIKE GREENBERG
WITH PAUL "HEMBO" HEMBEKIDES

HYPERION AVENUE
LOS ANGELES • NEW YORK

The authors would like to acknowledge Sports Reference, ESPN Research, and Greg Thompson of Hilldale Sports as invaluable resources for the research that went into this book. All statistics, records, and historical notes are accurate through the time of its first printing in April 2025.

First Edition, September 2025
10 9 8 7 6 5 4 3 2 1
FAC-004510-25191
Printed in the United States of America

Designed by Joshua Moore

Library of Congress Control Number: 2025934230
ISBN 978-1-368-10857-7
Reinforced binding

The authorized representative in the EU for product safety and compliance is Disney Trading B.V., Asterweg 15S, 1031 HL, Amsterdam, The Netherlands
email: DCP.DL-EU.bookscontact@disney.com

www.HyperionAvenueBooks.com

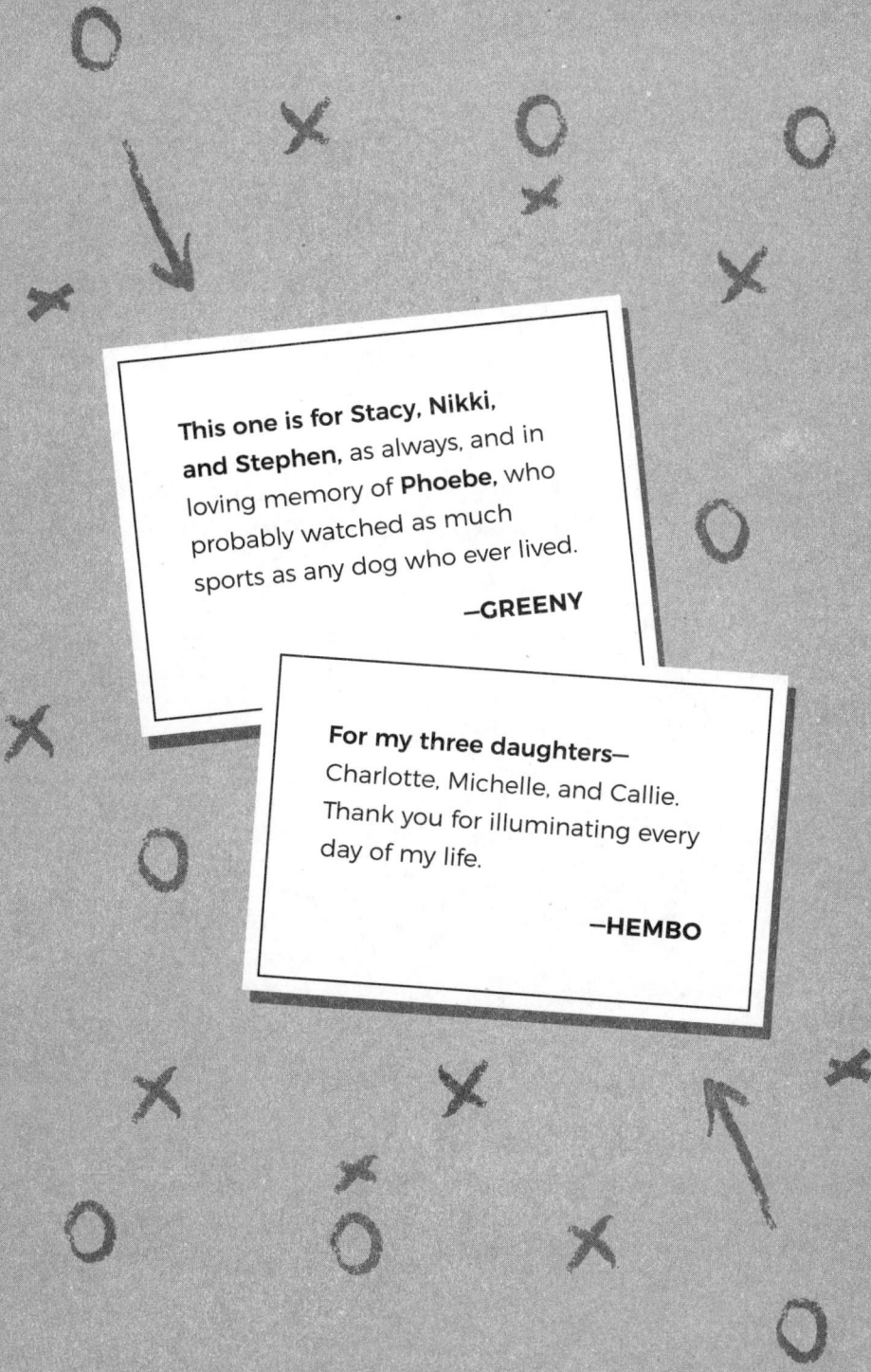

This one is for **Stacy, Nikki, and Stephen,** as always, and in loving memory of **Phoebe,** who probably watched as much sports as any dog who ever lived.

—GREENY

For my three daughters— Charlotte, Michelle, and Callie. Thank you for illuminating every day of my life.

—HEMBO

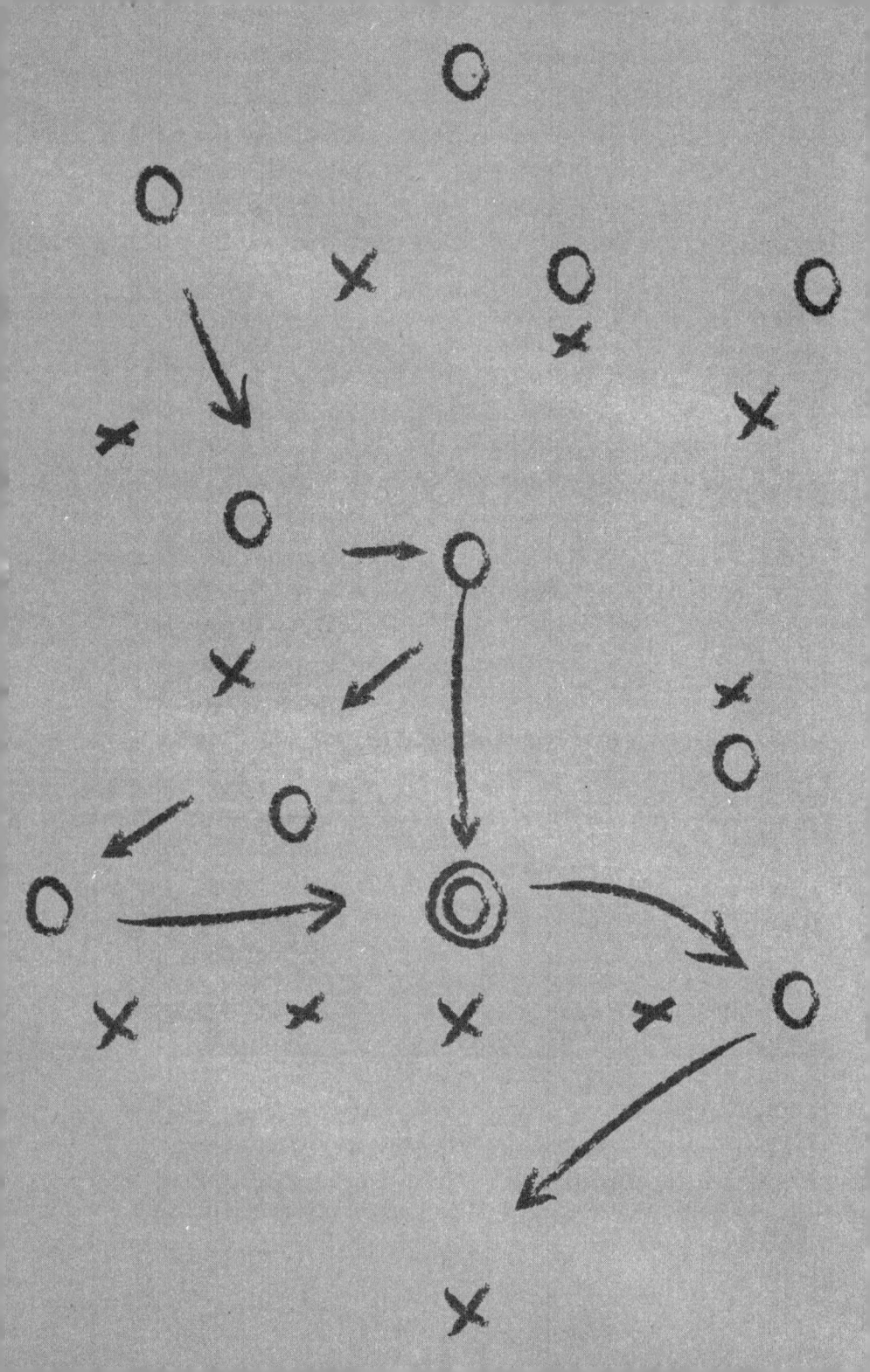

INTRODUCTION

T here are few more instantly recognizable images in the world than the visages carved into Mount Rushmore in the Black Hills near Keystone, South Dakota. Intended to symbolize the birth, growth, development, and preservation of the United States, the carved faces of George Washington, Thomas Jefferson, Theodore Roosevelt, and Abraham Lincoln have become as iconic a part of our national culture as the Statue of Liberty or the Lincoln Memorial. The group of faces have been portrayed in everything from Alfred Hitchcock's classic *North by Northwest* to the Rushmore Four who run the Presidents Race at every home game for baseball's Washington Nationals.

An unintended consequence of the selection of four faces to represent the nation has been a resulting tendency to use that number to choose the best in class of almost any category imaginable. Long before the Beatles were the Fab Four, people were debating the "Mount Rushmore" of everything from left-handed pitchers to virtuoso pianists. There is no other obvious reason to select the number four for such a designation; in a vacuum it seems as though either three or five would be more sensible and satisfying. But, in our culture today, right this minute, I guarantee there are a bunch of young people on a college campus debating who belongs on the Mount Rushmore of rock guitarists. Or rappers. Or quarterbacks. Not the top three, or the top five, but the four faces that represent the genre.

Nowhere does this conceit work more effectively than in sports. Over the three decades I have been hosting sports talk shows, it is likely I have concocted more than a thousand Mount Rushmores. So, when trying to come up with the concept for a book about the greatest legends in every team's history, Hembo and I knew there was only one way to do it. Thus, what follows could easily be described as the "Mount Rushmores of every team in the four major North American Sports Leagues." The fab four of every team, the faces of the franchises, chosen for their historical relevance, their competitive greatness, and their overall contributions to their teams.

Further, the order in which the franchises are listed is very much intentional, beginning at the apex and descending to the nadir, from the sublime to the ridiculous, beginning with the most successful and relevant franchises in American sports and finishing with the laughingstocks who deserve as much commentary from late night comedy hosts as they do anchors on *SportsCenter*. To be clear and fair to a lot of great individuals: What is being ranked is not the greatness of the franchise legends, but rather of the franchises themselves.

So, here come the legends and the franchises they made, in all their glory. I'm sure they will engender unanimous agreement, but in the unlikely event of any debate, I look forward to those discussions on the airwaves and internet more than I can put into words. Thank you, as always, for your support. Hembo and I sincerely hope you enjoy this one the most of all.

TIER 1

THE FABLED FOUR

1. Yankees
2. Celtics
3. Canadiens
4. Packers

TIER 2

THE ELECTRIC EIGHT

5. Lakers
6. Red Wings
7. Cardinals (MLB)
8. Steelers
9. Giants (MLB)
10. Patriots
11. Oilers
12. Bulls

TIER 3

THE SUPERB SIXTEEN

13. Dodgers
14. Spurs
15. Cowboys
16. 49ers
17. Penguins
18. Bruins
19. Bears
20. Giants (NFL)
21. Red Sox
22. Warriors
23. Athletics
24. Maple Leafs

TIER 4

THE THRILLING THIRTY-TWO

29. Browns
30. Blackhawks
31. Chiefs
32. Pirates
33. Rangers (NHL)
34. Braves
35. Tigers
36. Avalanche
37. Pistons
38. Ravens
39. Bucks
40. Knicks
41. Colts
42. Cubs
43. White Sox
44. Rockets
45. Lightning
46. Commanders
47. Devils
48. Thunder
49. Twins

TIER 5

THE FIELD OF SIXTY-FOUR

61. Astros
62. Dolphins
63. Trail Blazers
64. Flames
65. Raiders
66. Blue Jays
67. Pacers
68. Stars
69. Vikings
70. Ducks
71. Mets
72. Mavericks
73. Seahawks
74. Phillies
75. Capitals
76. Nets
77. Royals
78. Lions
79. Hawks
80. Canucks
81. Chargers
82. Angels
83. Cavaliers
84. Titans
85. Sabres
86. Kings (NBA)
87. Marlins
88. Hurricanes
89. Bills
90. Raptors
91. Diamondbacks
92. Predators
93. Buccaneers

TEAM RANKINGS

25. 76ers
26. Reds
27. Islanders
28. Heat

50. Eagles
51. Flyers
52. Nuggets
53. Rams
54. Guardians
55. Broncos
56. Jazz

57. Blues
58. Orioles
59. Kings (NHL)
60. Suns

94. Wizards
95. Panthers (NHL)
96. Rays
97. Saints
98. Nationals
99. Senators
100. Jets (NFL)
101. Rangers (MLB)
102. Magic
103. Cardinals (NFL)
104. Jets (NHL)

105. Brewers
106. Grizzlies
107. Bengals
108. Sharks
109. Clippers
110. Panthers (NFL)
111. Golden Knights
112. Mariners
113. Falcons
114. Wild
115. Timberwolves

116. Coyotes
117. Padres
118. Texans
119. Blue Jackets
120. Jaguars
121. Pelicans
122. Rockies
123. Hornets
124. Kraken

TIER

1

THE
FABLED
FOUR

—

Babe Ruth's popularity and fame were so wide-spread that even America's enemies knew of him. Almost a decade after he had bashed his last home run, his presence still was felt. During World War II, when Japanese soldiers charged American troops, they would sometimes scream, "To hell with Babe Ruth." Not "to hell with FDR" or "to hell with Douglas MacArthur," but "to hell with Babe Ruth." What bigger compliment could an American receive?

—Larry Schwartz, ESPN.COM

#1
NEW YORK YANKEES

✗ **Babe Ruth** ✗
✗ **Lou Gehrig** ✗
✗ **Joe DiMaggio** ✗
✗ **Mickey Mantle** ✗

O n this planet, or to my knowledge on any other, there is no symbol that emanates from the world of sports that is more universally recognizable than the interlocking NY on the front of a navy blue cap. I have seen it on the streets of every American city, amid the snake charmers in the Djemaa El Fna Square in Marrakech, Morocco, on bullet trains connecting Tokyo to Kyoto, Japan, and on the heads of countless celebrities attaching themselves to the power, prestige, and flat-out cool of the Yankees brand. *The New York Times* reported that the hat went viral in Brazil, where most of the populace is unaware it represents a baseball team, but rather think it "a classic piece of Americana." Which, indeed, it most certainly is.

In American sports, there are the Yankees—and then there is everyone else. That is true no matter the measurement, but most significantly in the most important category: winning. The Yankees have won twenty-seven World Series championships, seven more than their next two closest competitors combined. The Yankees also have, by a significant margin, the highest overall winning percentage in Major League Baseball history, having won 56.9 percent of their games; the Giants are next-best at 53.6 percent. There are also more players, managers, and broadcasters in the National Baseball Hall of Fame who have spent part or all of their careers with the Yankees than any other franchise; twenty-two Hall of Famers have been enshrined wearing a Yankees cap (the Giants/ Dodgers have the next most with fifteen) and, in all, there have been sixty-one players, managers, and executives inducted who had connections to the Yankees, along with seven broadcasters who have received the Ford C. Frick Award.

The Yankees have also had more iconic players than any other team in American sports history, which made their placement as the number one franchise an easy one, but the selection of their faces significantly challenging. Which is to say, the legends that do not make their Mount Rushmore might very well comprise a more impressive group than the first string of any other franchise. Consider, among others: Mariano Rivera, the greatest relief pitcher of all time and the only player ever unanimously voted into the Hall of Fame; Derek Jeter, the unquestioned face of the sport for two decades; Yogi Berra, the only ten-time World Series champion in baseball history; George Steinbrenner, perhaps the most outspoken, notorious, visible owner in the history of American sports; Joe

McCarthy and Casey Stengel, managers who each led the Yankees to seven World Series championships. Any of these legends, along with many others, would have been locks to make the cut for practically any other franchise in any sport.

However, as painful as leaving any of those off the list may have been, there remained four easy choices. With all due respect to the great Jay-Z, who rapped "I made the Yankee hat more famous than a Yankee can," that lyric does not apply to Babe Ruth, Lou Gehrig, Joe DiMaggio, or Mickey Mantle. Each of them is so well known, and so associated with the Yankees, that it hardly feels worth running through a list of their accomplishments. Merely consider that Ruth revolutionized the sport and remains the most famous player that ever lived, some nine decades after appearing in his final game. Gehrig describing himself to the Yankee Stadium crowd as "the luckiest man on the face of the earth" on July 4, 1939, remains the most famous speech in the history of American sports. He was also one of its most durable athletes, having played in 2,130 consecutive games from June 1, 1925 to April 30, 1939, a record that stood until Cal Ripken Jr. broke it in 1995. Joe DiMaggio's impact on the culture was so powerful that when Paul Simon endeavored to conjure the ideal symbol of American innocence lost, he wrote "Where have you gone, Joe DiMaggio, a nation turns its lonely eyes to you," a phrase that resonates to this day, with generations not nearly old enough to remember DiMaggio as a player. But a player he was: At his death, *The New York Times* called DiMaggio's 1941 56-game hitting streak "perhaps the most enduring record in sports." And, finally, the Mick, of whom Bob Costas said, "For millions of kids, Mickey Mantle was baseball." Even though more than fifty years have passed since Mantle's last at-bat, nobody has surpassed his record for most RBIs and home runs in the World Series.

Among a century's worth of legends, at least a dozen of whom would have topped the lists of practically any other team, this is the proper foursome to represent the most important franchise in all of sports.

#2
BOSTON CELTICS

The history of baseball has primarily been defined by one team; in basketball, it has been two. The Lakers and the Celtics are to the sport what Muhammad Ali and Joe Frazier once were to boxing—bigger than all the rest of them, combined. As of this writing, there have been seventy-eight NBA championships, and the two behemoths of basketball have combined for thirty-five of them (Celtics eighteen, Lakers seventeen)—that means 45 percent of the titles have been gobbled up by what currently amounts to less than 7 percent of the teams. The rivalry between the Lakers and Celtics is as storied, consequential, and respectfully hostile as any in sports, thus did a great deal of consideration go into which would be placed above the other here. In the end the Celtics get the nod, based more on their franchise history than the magnitude of their individual stars.

There has never been a National Basketball Association without the Boston Celtics as a member; one of the league's original teams, as of this writing, the Celtics have played in more games, and won more, than any team in NBA history. Their story is rich, complex, diverse, and highly accomplished. Of the first twenty-three championships earned in the sport, the Celtics won eleven. In 1950, the Celtics drafted Chuck Cooper out of Duquesne, making him the first Black player selected in league history. In 1966, Bill Russell became the first Black head coach in NBA history. It could be argued that there is no franchise more historically significant to any sport than the Celtics are to the NBA.

The logo of the Celtics has long been Lucky the Leprechaun, in honor of the city's heavily Irish American population. In truth, it could just as easily be the visage of Red Auerbach, the man who created the most dominant dynasty in the history of American pro sports. As the team's coach, with no formal assistants, Auerbach assembled and led the players. With the acquisitions of Bob Cousy, Bill Russell, Tom Heinsohn, Sam Jones, and K. C. Jones, among others, the Auerbach-led Celtics won nine championships before he stepped aside and handed the coaching reins to Russell in 1966. Auerbach went on to spend nearly four decades in the Celtics' front office, engineering the acquisitions of—among others—Dave Cowens, Jo Jo White, Larry Bird, Kevin McHale, and Robert Parish. In all, it could be argued that no non-player had a greater impact on the sport than Auerbach.

The accomplishments of Bill Russell are unmatched in

pro sports history, winning eleven championships in thirteen years as a player, and two of those as player-coach. In NBA history, only two players have won MVP in a title-winning season more than twice—Michael Jordan and Bill Russell, each doing so four times. His impact both on and off the floor cemented his place among the greatest legends our nation ever produced.

Far less heralded, or remembered, was his longtime teammate, John Havlicek. For reasons that have never been clear to me, Havlicek is among the least remembered immortals of basketball history. His defensive prowess (eight-time all-defensive team) enabled the Celtics to employ their famous full-court press. But he also scored more points in a Celtics uniform than Russell or Larry Bird, or any other Celtic for that matter. At the time of his retirement, he was third in NBA history in scoring and sixth in assists, and to this day he remains one of only two players who amassed 26,000 points, 8,000 rebounds, and 6,000 assists in their careers; LeBron James is the other.

As for Bird, his impact on the league cannot be measured simply by the titles (three) or MVPs (three in a row) that he won. Or even by his ridiculously long prime, finishing fourth, second, second, second, first, first, first, third, and second in MVP voting from 1980 to 1988. Rather, his most enduring feat is, along with his great rival, Magic Johnson, helping to elevate the sport, jump-starting the development of a league that went from having its championship round televised on tape delay to the global powerhouse it has subsequently become.

This Celtics foursome was another that was easy to choose but painful to depict, due to the omissions of such legendary stars as Cousy, Paul Pierce, and Heinsohn, who won eight championships with Boston as a player, two more as head coach, and was then a beloved member of the broadcast team for decades to follow. Any of those three would have been worthy of a space for almost any other franchise in the NBA, but these are the Celtics, after all, and they are most decidedly not just any other franchise.

#3
MONTREAL CANADIENS

For all but the most knowledgeable hockey fans, the history of the NHL traces back to the Original Six, the clubs that made up the league until it doubled in size in 1967. There were, however, several decades of professional hockey that came before, and right from the very outset, the most glamorous franchise was the Montreal Canadiens. Officially known as Le Club de Hockey Canadien, the Habs were founded in 1909 and stand as the oldest continuously operating professional ice hockey team on the planet. Despite a lengthy championship drought, they also remain overwhelmingly the most accomplished, winners of twenty-five championships (twenty-three Stanley Cups), which was the North American record until the Yankees won their twenty-sixth World Series in 2000.

Maurice Richard, originally nicknamed the Comet but now forever remembered as the Rocket, was among the NHL's first great stars. The captain of the dynastic teams of the 1950s, he led the Habs to an unprecedented five straight championships from 1956 to 1960. Quiet off the ice and fiercely combative on it, Richard was the first player ever to score fifty goals in a season and was the league's all-time leading scorer when he retired in 1960. Richard's younger brother, Henri, known as the Pocket Rocket, followed Maurice to the Canadiens; the two would combine to win nineteen Stanley Cups with the Canadiens, the most of any brothers in history, and are both enshrined in the Hockey Hall of Fame.

Jean Béliveau was another of the sport's most heralded early heroes, playing twenty seasons for the Canadiens, winning ten Stanley Cups, then seven more as an executive; his seventeen championships are the most in NHL history, and he won them all with Montreal. Such was Béliveau's enormous impact that he was made a Companion of the Order of Canada, the nation's highest civilian award, and in 2001 his portrait was used on a postage stamp.

The goaltender for Montreal's dynasty of the 1950s was Jacques Plante, whose brilliance, leadership, and innovation earned him his place on this list. Not only did Plante win six Stanley Cups and seven Vezina Trophies, but he also legitimately changed the face of the sport forever as the first goalie to wear a mask on a regular basis. Further, he was the first to direct his team in ways that have become commonplace today: exiting the crease to play the puck, going behind the net to stop it, and raising his arm on a potential icing call to alert his teammates.

Plante's uniform number 1 is one of fifteen numbers retired by Montreal, the most of any team in the NHL.

The Canadiens experienced another dynastic era in the 1970s, winning five Stanley Cups between 1973 and 1979, and the unquestioned star of those teams was Guy Lafleur. The first pick in the 1971 draft, Lafleur was heralded as the next Béliveau, and in practically every way lived up to the hype: He was the first player ever to score 50 goals in six straight seasons and remains the highest-scoring player in Montreal's history. However, it was his style and grace on the ice as much as his greatness that cemented his legend; when he died, Canadian outlet Sportsnet described Lafleur as "a Jackson Pollock painting on ice."

As a final word on the historical dominance of the Montreal Canadiens, consider that the President's Trophy, presented to the team that finishes the regular season with the most points, was first awarded in 1986. As of this writing, the Red Wings have won the award six times, the most of any franchise. However, had the trophy been awarded since the inception of the league, Montreal would have won it twenty-one times.

#4
GREEN BAY PACKERS

✕ **Vince Lombardi** ✕
✕ **Bart Starr** ✕
✕ **Brett Favre** ✕
✕ **Aaron Rodgers** ✕

There is no franchise in North American sports quite like the Green Bay Packers, not only because they represent (by far) the smallest home market of any team on the continent, but they are also the only nonprofit, community-owned major sports club in the United States. Yet, somehow, they have also managed to become the flagship franchise of America's most popular sport. The Packers have played in their original city longer than any other team in the NFL, and they are the league's most decorated club, with thirteen championships. The early days of the Packers were defined by two historical giants: Curly Lambeau and Don Hutson, the franchise founder and the superstar wide receiver respectively, who invented pass patterns that are still run today. Their omissions may have been the most challenging for any franchise across this entire project.

When any list of the great coaches is cobbled together, regardless of length, if it does not include Vince Lombardi then it simply does not deserve further examination. In fact, one might argue that football in this country can be divided into two sections: before and after the dynasty built by the combative genius from Brooklyn. Consider that in 1958, the season before Lombardi's arrival, the Packers finished 1–10–1, and the shareholders and community were so dispirited that the very existence of the franchise was believed to be in jeopardy. In their first year under Lombardi, the Packers' record jumped to 7–5. The local population was so excited that season tickets for the following year promptly sold out; every Packers home game played since then has been sold out. In Lombardi's second season, the Packers won the Western Conference championship for the first time since 1944, and then won back-to-back NFL titles in 1961 and 1962, the first of the five they would win in the decade—including the first two Super Bowls. In all, Lombardi would never have a losing season as head coach, and today, the most sought-after trophy in the sport (the Super Bowl championship trophy) bears his name.

The field general of Lombardi's dynastic squad is the first of the remaining three faces, the best trio any franchise has ever boasted at the game's most important position. Bart Starr was a seventeenth round selection out of Alabama, who went on to play sixteen years in Green Bay and remains the only quarterback ever to lead a team to three consecutive NFL championships. He was the MVP of each of the first two Super Bowls, and his postseason record of 9–1 remains the best in history.

The end of Starr's career began a lengthy title drought in "Titletown," as the Packers would struggle to find a worthy successor. When Brett Favre led Green Bay to the playoffs in 1993, his second year with the team, it was their first postseason appearance in more than a decade. What followed, of course, was an unprecedented period of brilliant quarterback play; with the combination of Favre and Aaron Rodgers at the helm, Green Bay would make the playoffs in twenty-two of twenty-nine seasons. Favre rewrote the NFL record books; at the time of his retirement, he was the league's all-time leader in passing yards, touchdowns, and quarterback wins. (His iron man record of 297 consecutive games started would, of course, include his stints with the Jets and Vikings.)

Upon his departure from Green Bay, Favre would hand the baton to Rodgers, who arguably reached even greater heights than his legendary predecessor. Rodgers would win four MVP Awards and one Super Bowl in Green Bay and is the franchise's all-time leader in completion percentage and touchdown passes. Rodgers held a variety of NFL records at the time of his departure from Green Bay as well, including the two highest-rated passing seasons in NFL history (2011 and 2020). There is no football franchise with three such superstars at the quarterback position, nor any with a history as storied or successful as the Packers; the tiny city of Green Bay, Wisconsin, can proudly boast the number one football franchise of them all.

TIER
2

THE
ELECTRIC
EIGHT

—

When we are saying this cannot be accomplished, this cannot be done, then we are short-changing ourselves. My brain—it cannot process failure. It will not process failure.

—Kobe Bryant, Los Angeles Lakers

5

LOS ANGELES LAKERS

⚔ **Jerry West** ⚔
⚔ **Kareem Abdul-Jabbar** ⚔
⚔ **Magic Johnson** ⚔
⚔ **Kobe Bryant** ⚔

The most glamorous franchise in all of American sports began in 1946 as the Detroit Gems of the National Basketball League, before relocating the following year to Minneapolis and being renamed the Lakers. In the earliest days of professional basketball, the Lakers were dominant, winning the NBL championship in 1948, then joining the rival Basketball Association of America in 1949 and winning the league title that season as well. In 1949 the leagues merged, forming the NBA as we know it today, and the Lakers were the first powerhouse, winning four of the next five NBA titles. By the 1960s, the team had relocated again, this time to Los Angeles. They qualified for the NBA Finals six times in the decade, and lost to the Celtics in all six trips, which is how a franchise this successful and beloved was relegated to second-tier status behind its forever rival.

However, when it comes to star power, the Lakers take a backseat to no one. Consider that when the league's fifty greatest players were named in 1996, Elgin Baylor, Shaquille O'Neal, George Mikan, and James Worthy were all selected, yet none of them warrant a place on the franchise's fab four. Neither does Wilt Chamberlain, despite winning a championship in a Lakers uniform in 1972; he played only the final five seasons of his iconic career in Los Angeles. Safe to say, any of those luminaries would have led the list of practically any other franchise, but among the Lakers legends there simply wasn't space.

It could be argued that Jerry West had as great a career as any person in any sport ever. His playing career lasted fourteen seasons (all of them with the Lakers), he was named an all-star fourteen times and first team All-NBA ten times, and was so iconic a player that in 1969 the NBA designed its logo to resemble his silhouette. After a largely successful three-year stint coaching the Lakers, West moved to the team's front office. As general manager, he built the dynastic Showtime squads of the 1980s, who were five-time champions and among the most charismatic collections any league has ever produced.

Those teams were led by Kareem Abdul-Jabbar and Magic Johnson, both of whom merit serious consideration for the Mount Rushmore of the entirety of basketball. Kareem played fourteen of his twenty NBA seasons for the Lakers and finished in the top five of the MVP voting in nine of them, winning three times. When he was joined by Johnson in the fall of 1979, the two proceeded to command one of the most consequential runs any team would ever enjoy; it is safe to say the Showtime Lakers brought as many people into the tent as any team in the history of the sport.

The final spot belongs to the late, great Kobe Bryant, who scored more points in a Lakers uniform than anyone else. In fact, only Karl Malone of the Jazz ever scored more points for any franchise than Kobe did for the Lakers. Bryant teamed with Shaq to form one of the most dominant duos of all time, winning three straight titles from 2000 to 2002, and then reinvented himself and the team as its centerpiece in winning two more at the end of that decade.

In all, these were painful decisions to have to make— but not difficult ones. The Lakers' list includes the second and fourth all-time leading scorers, the seventh all-time assists leader, the guy who *is* the NBA logo, all with sixteen championships as players among them. A finer foursome would be difficult to imagine. This group packs precisely the sort of star power that befits the Hollywood backdrop against which they played.

#6
DETROIT RED WINGS

* ✕ Gordie Howe ✕
* ✕ Terry Sawchuk ✕
* ✕ Nicklas Lidström ✕
* ✕ Steve Yzerman ✕

The game of ice hockey was first conceived, organized, and played in Canada during the second half of the nineteenth century. The first indoor game was played in 1875, in Montreal, utilizing dimensions for the rink and the puck that remain to this day. The sport became an instant obsession, as it indeed still is. The Stanley Cup—commissioned in 1892 to be awarded to the Canadian amateur champions—is among the most enduring and recognizable championship trophies in the world. As the sport's popularity has spread across the globe, its roots have remained firmly planted in Canada. Thus, it is appropriate that the two most decorated franchises in the NHL—the foremost hockey league on earth—represent that nation: the Montreal Canadiens and Toronto Maple Leafs. However, among all NHL franchises *not* based in Canada (currently twenty-five of the thirty-two play in the United States) the most successful, by a wide margin, has been the Red Wings. Winners of eleven Stanley Cups, the team has nearly twice as many as their nearest competitors, the Boston Bruins and Chicago Blackhawks, who each have six. For that reason, and because it boasts one of the NHL's Original Six teams, the city of Detroit has come to be referred to as Hockeytown.

From the inception of the franchise until the acquisition of their greatest star, the Red Wings won three championships over twenty years. When Gordie Howe arrived, everything changed. Mr. Hockey, as he will forever be known, hoisted the Stanley Cup four times in a six-year run, early in what would eventually be a twenty-five-year career in Detroit. Such was Howe's genius and impact that when, in 1998, the *Hockey News* listed him as the third greatest player ever, behind Wayne Gretzky and Bobby Orr, both Gretzky and Orr said they regarded Howe as number one.

Terry Sawchuk was the goalie for three of Howe's four championship teams, winning the Calder Trophy (best rookie) and three Vezina Trophies (top goalie) from 1951 to 1955, leading the league in wins in all five of those seasons. His uniform number 1 was retired by the Red Wings in 1994. His record for most career wins by a goalie (445) stood for thirty years after his retirement in 1970, and his record for most career shutouts (103) was finally surpassed by Martin Brodeur in 2009.

Swedish-born defenseman Nicklas Lidström played twenty years for the Red Wings, the final six of those as team captain. Detroit never missed the playoffs during Lidström's tenure, during which they won four Stanley Cups. Individually, Lidström won seven Norris Trophies as the league's top defenseman (only Bobby Orr won more) as well as the Conn Smythe in 2002 as the MVP of the postseason, the first European player ever to win that award.

Lidström was named the Red Wings' captain in 2006 upon the retirement of his longtime teammate, Steve Yzerman, who served in that capacity for two decades—the longest-serving team captain in North American sports history. Yzerman, often known as Stevie Wonder, won three Stanley Cups with Detroit, where he played all twenty-two of his NHL seasons. Yzerman remains in the top ten all-time in NHL history in points, goals, and assists, and currently serves as the team's vice president and general manager.

As with most of the older and more successful franchises, the Red Wings have featured multiple legends worthy of consideration for this book. Of special note among them is Jack Adams, who spent thirty-six years as either coach or general manager of the club, winning seven Stanley Cups in Detroit. He remains the only person to ever win the Stanley Cup as a player, coach, and general manager. Since 1974, the NHL's award for Coach of the Year has been known as the Jack Adams Award.

#7
ST. LOUIS CARDINALS

× **Stan Musial** ×
× **Bob Gibson** ×
× **Ozzie Smith** ×
× **Albert Pujols** ×

I have come across no persons from St. Louis who are not demonstrably proud of their hometown. When I ask why, invariably the first sentence of their reply will invoke their passion for "the Cards." Since the Cardinals' inception in 1882, it is possible there has been no city in America that has had a more meaningful love affair with its hometown team.

The first great era of the Cardinals organization was pioneered by Branch Rickey, who developed and led a business structure that revolutionized the sport. Rickey expanded scouting and player development, and created the first minor league farm system; in essence, he ushered in the structure that defines the operation of a baseball franchise to this day. Led by Rogers Hornsby, who won two Triple Crowns in the 1920s, and then the famous Gashouse Gang in the 1930s, the Cardinals became almost as dominant in the National League as their counterparts the Yankees were in the American League, winning five pennants and three World Series between 1926 and 1934.

That dominance has never been outdone in baseball; to date, the Cardinals have won eleven championships, a mark topped only by the Yankees.

Stan "the Man" Musial was among the most beloved and greatest players of his, or any, era. Musial retired holding at least a share of seventeen MLB records and twenty-nine NL records. Since his retirement, Tony Gwynn is the only player to finish with a higher career batting average, while Henry Aaron and Albert Pujols are the only ones to surpass Musial's 6,134 total bases. Musial also retired in second place on the NL's career home run list, with 475, and may have surpassed 500 had he not missed the 1945 season to serve in the US Navy in World War II. A statue of Musial was erected outside the ballpark in St. Louis in 1968, bearing the words *Here stands baseball's perfect warrior. Here stands baseball's perfect knight.*

In the 1960s, the Cardinals advanced to the World Series three times and won twice, with teams that featured dominating starting pitching, particularly by Bob Gibson, the most intimidating pitcher of his time. Gibson was the MVP of both those series; in all he started nine World Series games, finished eight of them, and won seven, allowing 17 earned runs and striking out 92 batters in 81 innings. Gibson's 1968 season may well have been the greatest in baseball history: His ERA was 1.12, he threw thirteen shutouts, and he completed twenty-eight of his thirty-four starts—he was pinch-hit for in the other six, meaning he was not removed for another pitcher the entire season.

Ozzie Smith (who only hit 28 home runs in his nine-teen MLB seasons) may be best remembered for his walk-off shot in Game 5 of the 1985 NLCS, which inspired announcer Jack Buck to tell the fans to "Go crazy, folks, go crazy!" However, what should be remembered about the Wizard of Oz is that he was inarguably the greatest defensive shortstop of all time, winner of thirteen Gold Gloves, and remains the all-time leader in shortstop assists.

The eleven seasons Albert Pujols spent in St. Louis to begin his career were among the most productive offensive stretches by any player in history. Pujols finished in the top five of MVP voting in ten of those years, winning the award three times, and hit 445 home runs as a Cardinal, leading St. Louis to two World Series championships.

As a final word, it should also be noted that the Cardinals have had two of the most enduring and endearing broadcasters in the game—either Jack Buck or Mike Shannon could easily have warranted a place on this list for the relationships they forged with the fans of Cardinal Nation, the most loyal and passionate fan base in the history of baseball.

#8
PITTSBURGH STEELERS

- ✕ **Chuck Noll** ✕
- ✕ **Joe Greene** ✕
- ✕ **Terry Bradshaw** ✕
- ✕ **Franco Harris** ✕

Today's football fans may be surprised to learn that, for what continues to amount to roughly 50 percent of their history, the Steelers were arguably the least successful franchise in the NFL. With roots that date back to a regional pro team in the 1920s, the Steelers are the seventh-oldest franchise in the sport, and the oldest that currently plays in the AFC. From 1933, when they officially joined the NFL as the Pittsburgh Pirates, until the merger in 1970, the Steelers qualified for the postseason only once, in 1947, losing their lone playoff game to the Eagles 21–0.

Everything began to change in 1969 with the hiring of Head Coach Chuck Noll and the selection of "Mean" Joe Greene in the draft. That was followed in short order by the selections of future Hall of Famers Terry Bradshaw and Mel Blount in 1970, Jack Ham in 1971, Franco Harris in 1972, and the legendary haul of 1974: Lynn Swann, Jack Lambert, John Stallworth, Mike Webster, plus undrafted free agent Donnie Shell—the only occasion in history where a team's rookie class included five Hall of Famers in a single year. Until the Steelers won Super Bowl IX, they were the oldest NFL team never to have won a championship. So began an era of dominance: The Steelers won four Super Bowls in six seasons, a feat that has never been matched since. Pittsburgh was transformed from one of the least successful franchises into arguably the most successful. Their six Super Bowl titles are tied for the most ever, while their eight Super Bowl appearances have been surpassed only by the Patriots.

Though Noll, Greene, Bradshaw, and Harris all represent the teams of the 1970s, they are this franchise's four faces, a decision not made casually. There have been excellent recent iterations of the Steelers, led by coaches Bill Cowher and Mike Tomlin, and featuring historically great players such as Ben Roethlisberger, Troy Polamalu, and Jerome Bettis. However, the Steel Curtain era was one of such dominance, and of such consequence to the growth of professional football in America, that players from those teams are more than worthy of occupying all four spaces. In fact, were there room for more faces, arguments could as easily be made for Lambert and Blount as for any player who came later. Those teams featured ten players, plus the owner, coach, and team president, who made the Hall of Fame. They remain the only team to win back-to-back Super Bowls *twice*. In the seventies, Pittsburgh made the playoffs in eight consecutive seasons, amassing a regular-season record of 88–27–1 during that stretch.

Noll's four Super Bowl titles are the most without a loss in NFL history, and second most overall behind only Bill Belichick. Bradshaw was a league MVP, two-time Super Bowl MVP, and winner of fourteen playoff games and four Super Bowls. His gap-toothed grin has been a fixture for football fans for more than half a century. Greene was the first cornerstone of the Steelers' dynasty and remained its best player: He was named to six All-Pro teams and was the NFL's Defensive Player of the Year twice. Harris rushed for nearly 12,000 yards in Pittsburgh, was MVP of the Steelers' first Super Bowl victory, made nine consecutive Pro Bowls, and boasts the most famous play in football history—the Immaculate Reception—to win a playoff game in 1972. These four men, and the legends they played with, changed everything, and not just in Pittsburgh. The Steelers' blue-collar image, juxtaposed against the flashy persona of their rival Dallas Cowboys, served to usher in the modern era of the NFL, transfixing the American public like never before, and transforming pro football from a moderately popular sideshow into the national obsession it has remained ever since.

#9
SAN FRANCISCO GIANTS

× **Christy Mathewson** ×
× **John McGraw** ×
× **Willie Mays** ×
× **Barry Bonds** ×

Consider America in 1883: The Brooklyn Bridge was opened, the world's first rodeo was held, the first vaudeville theater raised its curtain, and oxygen was liquified for the first time. Amidst all of these events, a baseball club called the New York Gothams was formed; two years later it was renamed the Giants. That team, New York's first professional franchise, has, to date, won more games than any other in all American sports, and has seen sixty-six players and managers enshrined in the National Baseball Hall of Fame—the most of any team in the sport. Playing at the Polo Grounds, the Giants won seventeen pennants and five World Series before relocating to San Francisco in 1958. The intracity rivalries between the Giants, Dodgers, and Yankees were as fierce and consequential as any in baseball history and remain the longest standing in American sports. Following the move west, the Giants would suffer a championship drought of longer than half a century before finally claiming World Series titles in 2010, 2012, and 2014. As of this writing, the Cardinals are the only National League team with more World Series championships, and the Dodgers the only one with more league pennants.

Along the way, star players for the Giants were responsible for many of the most enduring memories in baseball history. In 1922, manager John McGraw's team swept the Yankees in the World Series, limiting Babe Ruth to a .118 batting average and one RBI. In 1951, Bobby Thomson hit "the shot heard 'round the world," causing Russ Hodges to deliver perhaps the best-known play-by-play call of all time: "The Giants win the pennant! The Giants win the pennant!" Three years later, in Game 1 of the 1954 World Series at the Polo Grounds, Willie Mays made The Catch on a ball hit to very deep center field by Vic Wertz, generally regarded as one of the greatest defensive plays of all time.

McGraw and Mays are both easy choices to represent baseball's all-time winningest team. John McGraw managed the Giants for thirty-one seasons, winning ten pennants and three World Series. He ranks third on baseball's all-time wins list, behind only Connie Mack and Tony LaRussa. As for Mays, a strong argument could be made that he was the best baseball player who ever lived, doing everything on the field at the absolute highest level. Consider the combination of power and speed: Mays led the NL in home runs and stolen bases four times *each*. He also won twelve Gold Gloves playing center field, and still holds the record for the most putouts as an outfielder. In 1999, *The Sporting News* listed the top 100 players in baseball history, listing Mays second behind Babe Ruth. In 2015, President Barack Obama presented Mays with the Presidential Medal of Freedom.

Christy Mathewson pitched seventeen seasons for the Giants in the earliest days of the twentieth century and dominated the sport in ways that have seldom been approached, winning 373 games with a career ERA of 2.13. He threw three shutouts in the 1905 World Series—a record that will never fall—leading the Giants to their first title. When the first class was elected to baseball's Hall of Fame in 1936 it consisted of five players: Babe Ruth, Honus Wagner, Walter Johnson, Ty Cobb, and Christy Mathewson.

Finally, there is Barry Bonds, who remains baseball's most confounding player, perhaps ever, to quantify. Taken strictly at face value, his statistics suggest the greatest career in the history of baseball, yet it is hard to imagine even his most ardent defenders viewing them that way. Despite that, Bonds played fifteen of his twenty-two seasons for the Giants and was inarguably the most dominant offensive player of his generation—though we will never know with certainty how many of his peers used similar means to inflate their totals (and themselves). In the end, galling though some may find it, there is simply no way to tell the story of this iconic franchise without Bonds.

10

NEW ENGLAND PATRIOTS

Decades before Tom Brady was born, at a time when Bill Belichick was learning football at the knee of his father (a coach at the US Naval Academy), no one could have predicted that the Patriots would become the most glamorous franchise in football. The early years in New England were challenging, at best. The Patriots were the last of the eight teams formed to create the American Football League. Through the entire existence of the AFL, they never had a home stadium, playing their games in Fenway Park, Harvard Stadium, Nickerson Field (Boston University), and Alumni Stadium (Boston College)—all homes to more established sporting teams. The Patriots, now the standard-bearers for sporting excellence, failed to win a single postseason game from 1964 until 1985, a season in which they would qualify for their first Super Bowl, where they were trounced 46–10 by the Bears.

James Orthwein purchased the team in 1992 with the intention of moving it to his native St. Louis. To the ever-lasting betterment of football fans everywhere, he instead sold it to local businessman Robert Kraft, a Patriots fan since the team's inaugural season, and the rest—as they say—is history. Kraft oversaw the construction of Gillette Stadium, where, as of this writing, the team has sold out every game since 1994. As of 2024, the Patriots were ranked by *Forbes* as the third most valuable sporting franchise in the world.

Prior to what can fairly be described as the glory days in New England, the franchise could hang its hat on only one historically great player. Drafted fourth overall out of Alabama in 1973, guard John Hannah was described by *Sports Illustrated* as "the greatest offensive lineman of all time" just eight years later. Over the course of thirteen NFL seasons, Hannah was named an All-Pro ten times and was a member of the league's Teams of the Decade for the 1970s *and* the 1980s. In 1991, Hannah became the first Patriots player to be named to the Pro Football Hall of Fame. Hannah would retire after the 1985 season; his final game was Super Bowl XX.

It would be fifteen years after Hannah's retirement that the fortunes of the franchise would change forever with the hiring of Bill Belichick. In his second stint as a head coach, Belichick would lead the Patriots to a Super Bowl title in his second season. By the time his tenure in New England came to an end, Belichick would rewrite the record books, leading the Patriots to thirty post-season wins, six Super Bowl titles, and nine Super Bowl appearances. In the end, he owned a .500 or better record against *every single team* in the NFL during his 24 seasons in New England. All those accomplishments would come with Tom Brady at quarterback. Brady was drafted 199th by the Patriots the year Belichick arrived, and together, the two formed the most dominant duo in NFL history. Brady, too, would rewrite the record books in New England before departing for Tampa Bay for the final three seasons of his career; he won three league MVP awards and four Super Bowl MVPs as a Patriot. At the time of his retirement, Brady held practically every meaningful passing record in NFL history. Together, Brady and Belichick made nine Super Bowl appearances in 20 seasons, more than any other team across NFL history.

The fourth face of this franchise was Brady's favored target across the nine seasons they spent together in New England. Rob Gronkowski arrived via the second round of the draft in 2010 and immediately began compiling statistics no tight end had come close to; in all, he would catch seventy-nine regular-season touchdown passes and twelve more in the playoffs. (Brady and Gronkowski would reunite for two seasons in Tampa Bay; these statistics do not reflect their time together there.)

Led by Belichick, Brady, and Gronk, the Patriots went from being a largely unsuccessful franchise to the winningest in the NFL. Their six Super Bowl titles are tied for the most ever, while their eleven appearances stand alone at the top. During the Belichick/Brady era, the Patriots would have stretches in which they won twenty-one consecutive games, appeared in eight consecutive conference championship games, won eleven straight division titles, and posted a winning record in nineteen straight seasons. Nothing of the sort had ever been done before, and it is fair to wonder if we'll ever see anything quite like it again.

#11
EDMONTON OILERS

× **Wayne Gretzky** ×
× **Mark Messier** ×
× **Grant Fuhr** ×
× **Connor McDavid** ×

The World Hockey Association was founded in 1972 as a competitor to the NHL, the first organized attempt of that kind since the collapse of the Western Hockey League in 1926. The WHA originally featured twelve teams, but financial issues cut that number in half by 1978. In 1979 the league folded, and four of its teams were absorbed by the NHL. Remarkably, while it would be difficult to describe the WHA as a success, the final seasons of its existence saw it spawn the careers of several of the game's legends, including Mike Liut, Mike Gartner, Mark Messier, and Wayne Gretzky, the greatest hockey player who ever lived.

Of the four NHL teams that were born in the WHA, only one remains in its original location with its original name. The Edmonton Oilers—for whom Gretzky began his pro career in the WHA's final season—have never moved, while the original Winnipeg Jets became the Phoenix Coyotes, the Hartford Whalers became the Carolina Hurricanes, and the Quebec Nordiques became the Colorado Avalanche. The Oilers, meanwhile, not only survived but thrived, at least early on, in ways that very few teams ever have before or since. Led by Gretzky, Messier, Paul Coffey, Jarri Kurri, and Grant Fuhr, the Oilers won five Stanley Cups between 1984 and 1990. Despite the team's lack of success since, they remain tied for the most championships won by any team since the merger, and only the Canadiens have won more titles since the NHL's expansion in 1967.

As far as franchise faces are concerned, few teams can boast a collection of this magnitude. It begins with Gretzky, of course, whose best years came in Edmonton. Beginning with the organization's inaugural NHL season, the Great One won eight consecutive Hart Memorial Trophies as the league's most valuable player. Gretzky won the NHL's points title in all eight of those MVP seasons, totaling 1,520 in all. No other player in the NHL totaled more than 909 over that span (1980–87). In the team's second NHL season, he won his first of what would be seven straight Art Ross Trophies as the league's leader in points. Simply put, no player in any team sport was ever more individually dominant as Gretzky was during his tenure with the Oilers.

Regarding Messier, while he solidified his legend by captaining the 1994 New York Rangers to their first Stanley Cup in more than half a century, he too spent his greatest seasons in Edmonton. He starred on all five of the Oilers' title teams, the last of which came after Gretzky's departure.

Fuhr was in goal for the first four of Edmonton's championship seasons; he missed the fifth due to injury, though he was still on the team. In all, Fuhr played ten years for the Oilers, and, as the son of an Afro Canadian parent set a number of firsts in the NHL, including being the first Black player to win the Stanley Cup (1984), and the first inducted into the Hockey Hall of Fame in 2003.

The fourth face of the Oilers franchise is still nearer to the beginning than the end of his professional journey. However, there is no questioning Connor McDavid's place here; the first overall pick in the 2015 draft, he won his first Hart Trophy as league MVP in only his second season. In 2020–21, McDavid joined Gretzky as the only players ever to be unanimous choices for the Hart Trophy. Two seasons later, he would win his third, this time receiving 195 of 196 possible votes.

It should also be noted that the exclusion of Glen Sather from this group was among the more painful choices of the entire exercise. Sather served as either coach or general manager of the Oilers for twenty-three years and is widely credited with having convinced owner Peter Pocklington to acquire Gretzky. In later years, Gretzky would name his own father and Sather as his two most important mentors.

While the window of historic excellence was open only briefly for this franchise, the magnitude of what it accomplished in those seven seasons has only rarely been approached. The Oilers won five championships in that span, with two different players combining to win five MVPs, plus one Vezina Trophy and one Jack Adams Award. Perhaps best of all: During the NHL's centennial celebration in 2017, the 1984–85 squad was named the greatest team of all time, having lost only three playoff games in four series en route to the Stanley Cup title.

#12
CHICAGO BULLS

× **Jerry Krause** ×
× **Michael Jordan** ×
× **Phil Jackson** ×
× **Scottie Pippen** ×

The Chicago Bulls were founded in January 1966 and had amassed just seven winning seasons and won a total of three playoff series by the time the most important day in their history arrived. June 19, 1984, changed everything forever—not just in Chicago but across the globe. The NBA Draft was held that day in Madison Square Garden, and the Bulls had the third pick. Everyone knew the Rockets would take center Hakeem (then Akeem) Olajuwon with the number one pick, and it would be hard to argue even now that they made a mistake. It was the Trail Blazers selecting big man Sam Bowie second (because they already had a dynamic shooting guard in Clyde Drexler) that opened the door for the Bulls. As Shakespeare wrote, "Some are born great, some achieve greatness, and others have greatness thrust upon them." On that night, the Chicago Bulls had greatness thrust upon them. They chose Michael Jeffrey Jordan with the third pick, and it is not an overstatement to say the world has never been the same.

The decade of the 1990s belonged to the Bulls, in general, and Jordan, in particular, in a way that few decades have ever been owned by any sporting organization, before or since. They won six championships, a feat even the New York Yankees have matched only once (in the 1950s) and never surpassed. The Montreal Canadiens won six Stanley Cups in the 1970s, which is the most in NHL history. No NFL team has ever done it. Only the Boston Celtics of the 1960s, led by Bill Russell, won more than six championships; otherwise put, Michael Jordan's Bulls authored a decade of dominance that has only ever been surpassed once in the history of American major sports.

It is for that reason that all four of this franchise's faces must represent that era, despite the worthiness of several other players, most notably Hall of Famer Bob Love and hard-nosed guard Jerry Sloan (both of whom had their numbers retired by the franchise), as well as Derrick Rose, who was the league MVP in 2011.

Jordan is the obvious first choice—if you need that explained to you, you are probably reading the wrong book. Consider that Magic Johnson, himself among the handful of greatest players in the history of the sport, famously said, "There's Michael Jordan, and then there's the rest of us."

Scottie Pippen is just as easy a selection for this list— arguably the greatest Robin to any Batman in sports history. His diverse, athletic skill set perfectly complemented

Jordan's enormous presence. Pippen was an elite wing with enough length to defend four positions, while slashing to the basket and spreading the floor with outside shooting. I covered the Bulls of 1993–94, while Jordan was in his first retirement, and I will forever believe Pippen should have been named the league MVP that season. Simply put, the Bulls don't win any of those six titles without him. The fact that he seems to have emerged from the experience feeling bitter and hurt is, in my mind, a sports tragedy.

Phil Jackson and Jerry Krause (the man who plucked Jackson from the obscurity of the Continental Basketball Association) round out this list as the other mainstays and integral pieces of all six championship teams. Jackson is, of course, equally remembered for the additional five championships he won with the Lakers, but it was in Chicago that he became a legend. Having covered those teams, I have frequently been asked some variation on "Wouldn't any coach have won with Michael Jordan?" My answer is always the same. "Yes, probably, once. Not every single time." It is worth noting, in fact, that had Michael not retired after the 1993 Finals, the Bulls may very well have won more titles. (In Chicago, we are fond of saying, *Minimum eight-peat, my friend.*)

As for Krause, his clashes with Jordan, Pippen, and Jackson may or may not have hastened the breakup of the Bulls. Meanwhile, his cantankerous manner and disheveled appearance made him an easy target for those inside and outside the organization. But the irrefutable truth is that he did a brilliant job managing the roster during those championship years; there is no way the Bulls would have done that amount of high-level winning without him. Among his most impactful moves were acquiring both Scottie Pippen and Horace Grant in the 1987 draft, trading Will Perdue for Dennis Rodman, hiring Phil Jackson away from the CBA's Albany Patroons, and adding players like Ron Harper, Steve Kerr, Luc Longley, and Trent Tucker who played vital roles in the team's continued success. For his part, Rodman led the league in rebounding all three seasons he was with the Bulls, the three highest rebound-ing seasons in franchise history. That Krause was not inducted into the Hall of Fame before his death was a gross injustice; he richly deserved his place and should have been able to appreciate the capstone of his career.

Before and after the Jordan era, the Bulls' history has largely been forgettable—what is certain is that no one who was alive to see it could ever forget what this team accomplished in the 1990s. Because of that era alone, the franchise deserves this high a place in the history of sports.

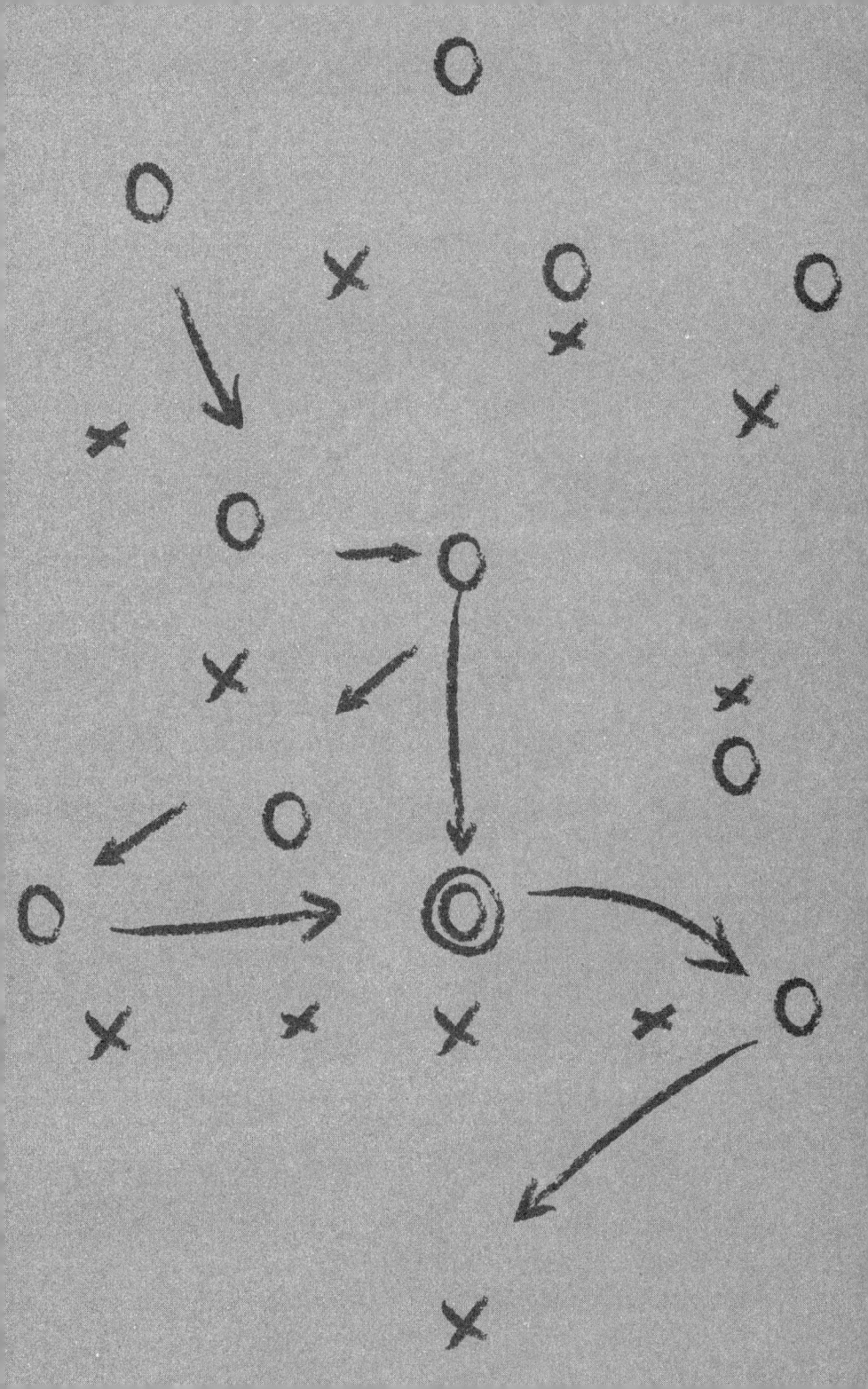

THE
SUPERB
SIXTEEN

—

From the Romans to the Native Americans to the U.S. Marine Corps, the battle cry remains the primary method of pushing the fear down so far the whimpering can't be heard. On the football field, there was no one louder than me.

—Dick Butkus, Chicago Bears

#13
LOS ANGELES DODGERS

⚒ **Jackie Robinson** ⚒
⚒ **Vin Scully** ⚒
⚒ **Sandy Koufax** ⚒
⚒ **Clayton Kershaw** ⚒

I f you ask those who were alive to see it, most of them will tell you that there has never been anything in sports quite like the intracity baseball rivalries between the New York Yankees, New York Giants, and Brooklyn Dodgers. For most of the first century of baseball's history, the city was the epicenter of the sport and showcased the game's biggest celebrities, particularly in the 1950s, when New York's center field trio of Willie Mays, Mickey Mantle, and Duke Snider were baseball's version of the Holy Trinity. While it was the Yankees who usually came out on top, the Dodgers were nearly always right behind, and even after they moved to Los Angeles and forged an identity all their own, they have always remained among the most successful—and glamorous—teams in all of sports.

As of this writing the Dodgers have won eight World Series and a National League record twenty-five pennants (and another in the American Association). They have featured eight Cy Young winners who captured a total of twelve awards, the most of any franchise. They have also produced eighteen Rookie of the Year winners, twice as many as any other team. Further, and perhaps most remarkably, from 1954 through 1996, the Dodgers had only two managers: Walter Alston and Tommy Lasorda. Between them, the two managed 6,698 games, winning 3,639 and six of the franchise's seven championships. The exclusion of both these iconic leaders was painful, as was that of Branch Rickey, the general manager who signed Jackie Robinson and paved the way for the breaking of the color barrier, which will always be the most significant event in the sport's history.

Robinson, of course, leads the way, with accomplishments too numerous to mention. Outside of statistics, he was the first Dodger to be honored with a statue; his uniform number 42 was the first one retired across any of the four major professional sports leagues; and he was one of the first athletes to receive the Presidential Medal of Freedom.

Sandy Koufax overlapped with Robinson for the first two of the pitcher's twelve seasons with the Dodgers. (Koufax never pitched in the minor leagues; the Dodgers were his only professional team.) Koufax won the Major League Triple Crown (wins, ERA, strikeouts) three times (1963, 1965, 1966), leading the Dodgers to a pennant in each of those years. He was the first pitcher to throw four no-hitters, including a perfect game in 1965, and was named MVP of the World Series twice.

Clayton Kershaw's career arc has been much longer than that of Koufax, and every bit as dominant. Kershaw is a three-time Cy Young winner, a World Series champion, and the 2014 National League MVP. Kershaw's lack of postseason success has been even more confounding when juxtaposed against the absolute brilliance of his career. Were his postseason record (13–13, 4.49 ERA) even remotely comparable to his regular-season numbers (2.49 ERA), there would be a legitimate argument to be made that he has been baseball's best pitcher to debut in the live-ball era (since 1920).

Vin Scully rounds out this formidable foursome, as the universally acknowledged GOAT of sports announcers. Scully's longevity (sixty-seven years as the voice of the Dodgers) speaks for itself—but only if it speaks in his voice does it tell the full story. Scully's career began when the Dodgers were still in Brooklyn and ended with his being honored with the Presidential Medal of Freedom in 2016. For an announcer to crack the list of a franchise with such a rich legacy tells the story; the truth is, there is no way to tell the story of the Dodgers without Vin Scully, and there is no one you'd rather have telling it either.

#14
SAN ANTONIO SPURS

✕ **George Gervin** ✕
✕ **Gregg Popovich** ✕
✕ **David Robinson** ✕
✕ **Tim Duncan** ✕

The San Antonio Spurs joined the NBA as part of the 1976 merger with the American Basketball Association, and it could be argued that over the entirety of their tenure in the league, they have been the second most successful franchise in the sport. In that time, only the Lakers and Michael Jordan's Bulls have won more than the five championships the Spurs have brought home to San Antonio. The Spurs were excellent from the outset. Despite prohibitive rules that made it harder for the newly added teams, the Spurs won forty-four games in their first NBA season and, led by Hall of Famer George Gervin, captured five division championships in the first seven years after the merger. Far greater success would arrive a generation later, when the franchise drafted two historically great big men: David Robinson in 1987 and Tim Duncan ten years later. The pair would capture NBA titles together in 1999 and 2003, after which Duncan would lead the way to three more over the following eleven years.

The sustained excellence of the Spurs has extended well beyond their championship seasons. The Spurs own the second-highest win percentage in the NBA since the merger, sandwiched between the Lakers and the Celtics. From 1999 through 2017, they strung together a record eighteen consecutive fifty-win seasons, part of a run of twenty-two consecutive years making the playoffs, matching the all-time NBA record. While the franchise has fallen on harder times in more recent years, the selection of French phenom Victor Wembanyama in the 2023 draft placed San Antonio back squarely in the mix of the most important NBA teams and suggests a future bright enough to mirror the past.

Gervin is, quite literally in fact, the first face of this franchise, taking the NBA by storm in the very first season after the merger; Gervin was an all-star that year, and each of the eight that followed. Despite the brilliance of the Spurs championship teams a generation later, his career scoring average of 26.3 points per game remains the highest in Spurs history. In the (unfairly) oft-forgotten era of 1970s basketball, Gervin was one of the league's most dynamic superstars.

Duncan, of course, stands above the rest as one of the most respected and accomplished players in the history of the game. Playing his entire career with the Spurs, he was a five-time champion, three-time Finals MVP, and two-time league MVP, being named All-NBA first team ten times. A strong argument could be made that on the all-time NBA starting five Duncan would be the power forward.

Duncan's teammate David Robinson is an easy choice for inclusion, as well. The Admiral, as he was known, made an immediate impact upon arriving from his two-year commitment to naval service. He won Rookie of the Year in 1990 and never looked back, being named MVP in 1995, earning ten all-star selections, and winning his second championship in his final NBA game.

The mastermind behind all five of the Spurs championships is Hall of Fame coach Gregg Popovich, who has also served as the team's president. The winningest coach in NBA history and a three-time NBA Coach of the Year, Coach Pop is the longest-tenured active head coach of any team in American sports. His legacy began with a record twenty-two consecutive winning seasons, and he is one of only five coaches to win as many as five NBA titles.

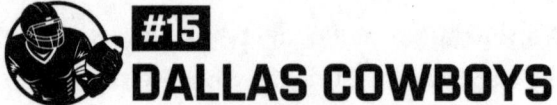

#15
DALLAS COWBOYS

✕ **Tom Landry** ✕
✕ **Roger Staubach** ✕
✕ **Jerry Jones** ✕
✕ **Emmitt Smith** ✕

In 1952, the Dallas Texans folded after just one season of play. Thus there was no NFL team south of the nation's capital until 1960, when an oil man named Clint Murchison founded the Dallas Cowboys. Before they had scheduled a game, he hired network executive Tex Schramm as team president and then–New York Giants defensive coordinator Tom Landry as head coach, and professional sports in this country would never be the same again.

The Cowboys would soon come to be known as America's Team, featuring the nation's most famous cheerleaders on the sideline, and one of the NFL's best assemblage of athletes on the field. In the 1970s, the Cowboys won more games than any other franchise and appeared in five Super Bowls, winning two. Everything about the look and feel of the franchise seemed to reso-nate, from the stars on the helmets to the fedora worn by its legendary coach. Change came in a big way in 1989, when businessman Jerry Jones bought the Cowboys and installed Jimmy Johnson as head coach. Another decade of dominance would ensue: three more Super Bowl wins in four seasons from 1992 to 1995. A personality conflict between Jones and Johnson hastened the coach's departure after the second of those championships, and before long the team's successful run would stall. As of this writing, Dallas has not advanced even to the conference championship game since the 1995 season. But that lack of winning has not kept Jones from turning the Cowboys into the most valuable sports franchise in the entire world; the team he purchased for $140 million in 1989 was valued by Sportico at $10.3 billion in 2024.

Landry is an easy choice for this list, despite the brilliance of so many players that miss the cut. For as great and legendary as Troy Aikman, Michael Irvin, Bob Lilly, Tony Dorsett, and a host of other Hall of Famers may have been, none of them defined the entire sport for two generations of fans. Tom Landry most certainly did; the image of him in a suit, tie, and hat may as well have been the NFL logo in the 1970s. There was, of course, an endless supply of substance behind the coach's style: His Cowboys made the playoffs eighteen times in a twenty-season stretch, reaching five Super Bowls and winning two; his innovative Flex defense revolutionized the sport and perplexed offensive coordinators in the 1960s. Even his coaching tree was abundant, as seven of Landry's assistants became NFL head coaches, including Mike Ditka and Dan Reeves.

The man who unceremoniously fired Landry also deserves to have his face on this tableau, for better or for worse. Jerry Jones has been among the most powerful, visible, and influential owners in sports over the past three decades, despite practically all his on-field success coming in one rapid burst in the earliest days of his tenure. Jones was the first in league history to win three Super Bowls within his first seven years of ownership. Upon installing himself at the top of the personnel department, though, Jones would see his team fall off precipitously, hence the decades of absence from the sport's largest stages. His leadership on issues of business and marketing, however, have taken a backseat to no one; Jones is universally credited as being among the primary drivers of pro football's dramatic ascendancy in revenue and relevance, particularly on television.

The Cowboys have thirty-two players in the Pro Football Hall of Fame, of whom sixteen are also in the team's Ring of Honor. Selecting only two of those is a harrowing exercise, although not an especially complicated one in the end. The Cowboys' history of success can be neatly divided into two time periods—the first of which was defined on the field by Roger Staubach, and the second by Emmitt Smith. Staubach was nicknamed Captain America and was the perfect post-Vietnam sports hero: a Heisman winner at Navy who served in the war before beginning his eleven-year career with the

Cowboys, leading Dallas to four Super Bowls and earning six Pro Bowl selections. He remains one of two quarterbacks to win the Heisman and be named MVP of the Super Bowl (Jim Plunkett is the other). He was voted NFL Man of the Year in 1978, an award that is today named for the legendary Walter Payton.

It is, of course, Payton's all-time rushing record that Emmitt Smith eventually broke. (He remains the only player with more yards than Payton.) Smith was the main cog in the Cowboys' 1990s dynasty, winning the league's MVP award in 1993 and a Super Bowl MVP as well. Smith played thirteen seasons in Dallas and scored more touchdowns as a Cowboy than any other running back has ever scored for any team. The rosters he played on were loaded, with both talent and personality, but Smith was always the most important piece.

The value of the franchise tells some, but not all, of the story with the Cowboys. They have become the most important team in American sports in any number of ways: Their impact on television ratings, revenue, and relevancy are unmatched. Critics will argue they do it at the expense of winning, which I think is foolish; one has little or nothing to do with the other. They were America's Team when they were winning championships, too. Success on the field will always ebb and flow, but the Cowboys' run of glamor and pertinence currently shows no sign of slowing down.

#16
SAN FRANCISCO 49ERS

× **Bill Walsh** ×
× **Joe Montana** ×
× **Ronnie Lott** ×
× **Jerry Rice** ×

I f you've never heard of the All-America Football Conference (AAFC) you are not alone; the upstart competitor to the NFL lasted just a few seasons, a very long time ago (1946–49). However, the AAFC had an impact on football that is very much felt to this day, giving birth to two franchises that continue to define pro football: the Cleveland Browns and the San Francisco 49ers.

Both teams joined the NFL in 1950 after the AAFC merged with the NFL, but, while the Browns would enjoy immediate success, the Niners mostly struggled for the better part of three decades. It was the hiring of coach Bill Walsh and the selection of quarterback Joe Montana— both in 1979—that turned those fortunes around; the Niners soon emerged as one of the most dominant teams in the NFL and have largely remained so since.

Led by Walsh and Montana, the Niners won their first Super Bowl in the 1981 season and experienced continued success throughout the decade, winning four Super Bowls over the next decade. Walsh's innovative offensive schemes, known as the West Coast Offense, revolutionized the game and helped the Niners become a powerhouse. In the 1990s, the 49ers remained highly competitive, battling with Dallas through most of the decade, and winning Super Bowl XXVIII under head coach George Seifert. The "down" years that followed the retirement of Hall of Fame quarterback Steve Young were comparatively short-lived; the franchise enjoyed some success behind quarterback Jeff Garcia and head coach Steve Mariucci in the early aughts, and then in 2011 hired Jim Harbaugh as head coach, ushering in a new era of success. Behind a strong defense and the emergence of quarterback Colin Kaepernick, the team reached Super Bowl XLVII, falling short against Harbaugh's brother, John, and the Ravens. More recently, the combination of general manager John Lynch and head coach Kyle Shanahan have made San Francisco the class of the NFC, reaching two Super Bowls and falling just short against Patrick Mahomes and the Chiefs both times.

The faces of this franchise all represent the first era of San Francisco's success: teams that were as dominant, innovative, and influential as practically any in football history. It begins with Walsh and Montana together, as there is no way to tell the story of either legend without the other. The two dominated, and revolutionized, the game with the West Coast Offense, which is characterized by short, precise passes and a quick tempo. Elements of that offense are still present across the NFL decades later. Their collaboration led to three Super Bowl victories in the 1980s seasons, cementing the Niners' dynasty. This legendary partnership exemplified synergy, where the coach's vision and the players' execution harmonized to achieve unprecedented success and leave an enduring legacy in the annals of football history.

Ronnie Lott was a rookie on the first of those Super Bowl teams and defined the toughness of a defense that dominated the sport. He would win four championships in his decade in San Francisco, intercepting nine balls in twenty postseason games, earning ten Pro Bowl selections and six first-team All-Pro nods during his career.

As for Jerry Rice, there simply isn't enough space to list all the accomplishments and accolades of his career; he remains—by a wide margin—the most accomplished and respected wide receiver who ever lived. Rice tops the list for career receptions (1,549), receiving yards (22,895), receiving touchdowns (197), and yards from scrimmage (23,540). Rice also held the record for Super Bowl receptions (33) until recently and retains the record for Super Bowl receiving yards (589), the overwhelming majority of which came in a Niners uniform. In fact, all three of the legendary players selected here finished their careers with other franchises—but there is no debate that each will forever be remembered for their role in San Francisco's dynasty, a run as noteworthy as any in NFL history.

#17
PITTSBURGH PENGUINS

⚔ **Mario Lemieux** ⚔
⚔ **Jaromír Jágr** ⚔
⚔ **Sidney Crosby** ⚔
⚔ **Evgeni Malkin** ⚔

Today, the very concept of the NHL's 1967 expansion, in which a professional sports league literally doubled in size in a single offseason, seems too far-fetched to be true. It was the largest expansion ever in any of the major sports leagues, and the first change to the composition of the NHL since 1942, ending the era of the Original Six. Thus, it seems reasonable to divide hockey history into two periods: before and after 1967. And, in the expansion era, no team has done more high-level winning than the Pittsburgh Penguins.

The earliest years in Pittsburgh were notable mostly for the team's struggles, both financially and on the ice. However, just as hockey's history can be divided in two pieces, so too can Pittsburgh's: before and after the Penguins' addition of Mario Lemieux. Super Mario's arrival heralded a new era for Pittsburgh: He led the team to back-to-back Stanley Cup championships in 1991 and 1992, establishing the Penguins as a force in the NHL and solidifying his status as one of the game's all-time greatest players. Despite further financial struggles in the late 1990s, Lemieux's leadership both on and off the ice kept the Penguins competitive. (And his return from retirement in 2000 provided a much-needed boost.) In 2005, the Penguins would draft Sidney Crosby, another generational talent who reshaped their trajectory. Under Crosby's captaincy, the Penguins won three Stanley Cups in 2009, 2016, and 2017—those back-to-back championships were the league's first in the salary cap era. Pittsburgh's five titles are tied with the Oilers for the most among teams not in the Original Six.

Lemieux is the obvious first choice to represent the franchise he literally saved. He not only spent his entire playing career in Pittsburgh, he also rescued the Penguins from bankruptcy in the late 1990s by leading the team to financial stability. He remains the only man to have his name on the Stanley Cup as both a player and an owner.

Sid the Kid is next up in Pittsburgh, the first overall pick in 2005, who announced his presence instantly: In only his second season, he led the NHL with 120 points to capture the Art Ross Trophy, becoming the youngest player—and only teenager—ever to win a scoring title in any of the major pro sports leagues.

As Lemieux was carrying the Penguins to greater heights, he needed a sidekick, and Jaromír Jágr arrived at the perfect time. At age twenty, Jágr became one of the youngest players to score a goal in the Stanley Cup Final.

In all, Jágr would play 806 games with Pittsburgh, becoming just the second Penguin to score 1,000 points for the franchise and ultimately just the third to have his number (68) retired.

Rounding out the foursome is longtime center Evgeni Malkin, three-time Stanley Cup champion and 2009 Conn Smythe winner. Malkin, still going strong as of this writing, has surpassed Jágr in all-time points for the Penguins, and now trails only Lemieux and Crosby.

Malkin was the second pick in the 2004 draft, and thus the perfect complement to the group he joins: Lemieux and Crosby were both selected number one, Jágr number five. The Penguins earned all their titles the old-fashioned way: by hitting on their highest draft picks, choosing and developing these stars into four of the greatest players in the history of the sport.

#18
BOSTON BRUINS

⚑ Eddie Shore ⚑
⚑ Bobby Orr ⚑
⚑ Phil Esposito ⚑
⚑ Ray Bourque ⚑

More than twenty years before there were the Boston Celtics, and nearly forty years before there were the Boston (now New England) Patriots, Boston's Original Six franchise joined the NHL. The Bruins debuted in the NHL's 1924–25 season and, though they struggled in the early years, quickly became a force to be reckoned with. In 1929, under the leadership of coach Art Ross, the Bruins defeated the Rangers in the Final to win their first Stanley Cup. This marked the beginning of a dominant run; throughout the 1930s—boasting a lineup that included such legends as Milt Schmidt, Woody Dumart, Roy Conacher, Dit Clapper, and Bobby Bauer—the Bruins would clinch two more titles in 1939 and 1941, establishing themselves as one of the league's powerhouse franchises. The Bruins have won six Stanley Cups in all, tied with the Blackhawks for second most among American-based teams, trailing only the Red Wings.

Chronologically, Eddie Shore is the first face of this franchise. From 1926 to 1939, the defenseman epitomized skill-driven toughness: winning four Hart Memorial Trophies as the league's most valuable player (a record for defensemen), tallying 103 goals and 176 assists for Boston, while also amassing 1,090 penalty minutes in 541 games. His legacy extends well beyond statistics, shaping the role of defensemen and influencing the game's physicality.

The greatest defenseman in Boston—or any team's—history, of course, is Bobby Orr, who revolutionized the position with his unparalleled skill and speed. Orr reimagined what was possible at the position, and amassed endless accolades, including eight Norris Trophies as the NHL's best defenseman and three Hart Trophies as MVP. Orr led the Bruins to Stanley Cup victories in 1970 and 1972, earning the Conn Smythe Trophy both times. With 888 points in 631 games for Boston, Orr is viewed by many as the second-greatest hockey player of all time, behind only Wayne Gretzky.

Phil Esposito's tenure with the Bruins, from 1967 to 1975, was monumental. The prolific center shattered scoring records—clinching five Art Ross Trophies as the league's top scorer, exceeding 100 points in a season six times—and led the Bruins to two Stanley Cups in 1970 and 1972. His 76 goals in the 1970–71 season stood as the NHL record for over a decade, broken by Wayne Gretzky.

Esposito is the exception for a franchise that has always been defined by its defensemen, and from 1979 to 2000 it was defined by Ray Bourque. Scoring 395 of his goals and 1,111 of his assists as a Bruin, Bourque remains the highest-scoring defenseman in NHL history. He won five Norris Trophies and, despite never winning a Stanley Cup with the franchise, his leadership and brilliance on the ice rendered him an iconic figure in Boston sports history.

#19
CHICAGO BEARS

× **George Halas** ×
× **Mike Ditka** ×
× **Dick Butkus** ×
× **Walter Payton** ×

The year 1919 was a tumultuous and significant one in the United States: Prohibition began, the toaster was invented, and the Chicago "Black Sox" threw the World Series, casting the credibility of the entire sports world into doubt. That same year, the owner of the A. E. Staley food starch company founded a company football team, known as the Decatur Staleys. George Halas took over the team, moved it to Chicago in 1921, and then renamed it the Bears the following year. Under Halas (either as coach or executive or both), the Bears won eight championships between 1921 and 1963. In 1985, they would achieve one of the greatest seasons in football history, demolishing everything in their path to finish the regular season 15–1 and winning the only Super Bowl championship in franchise history. The Bears have a tradition as rich as that of any team in pro football, illustrated by their record thirty-two players enshrined in the Hall of Fame.

Halas, known as Papa Bear, is where the franchise

begins. He was an innovative coach, introducing the T-formation, which revolutionized offensive strategies. His coaching prowess led to 324 career wins (including playoff games), which was the all-time record at the time of his retirement and remains third most to this day. Halas's contributions extended off the field as well, cofounding the NFL and pushing for its growth. His impact on the sport's development and success is immeasurable, cementing his place as one of football's most influential figures.

The star of the 1963 championship team was a tight end Halas drafted out of Pittsburgh in 1961 named Mike Ditka. Iron Mike made five Pro Bowls in his six seasons with Chicago, and then returned to the franchise as head coach after his playing career ended. Ditka would coach the Bears for eleven seasons, winning 106 games, six division titles, and a championship in Super Bowl XX. In 2013, Ditka's number 89 was retired by the franchise in an emotional ceremony at Soldier Field. He finished his speech by shouting "Thank you! Thank you! Thank you! And go Bears!"

The Bears—known as the Monsters of the Midway—have always been a franchise built on defense, and in their century-long history there has never been a monster as scary as linebacker Dick Butkus. In fact, from 1965 to 1973, there were no two more intimidating words in all of sports. His career, though cut short by knee injuries, was marked by ferocious tackling and unmatched intensity. He totaled 22 interceptions and 27 fumble recoveries, was selected to eight Pro Bowls, earned six first-team All-Pro honors, and was twice named Defensive Player of the Year. Butkus was inducted into the Hall of Fame in 1979 (his first year of eligibility), and in 1994, his uniform number 51 was retired by the Bears.

The man known as Sweetness, Walter Payton, a versatile running back possessing speed, agility, and incredible durability, played all thirteen of his seasons in Chicago. Payton's career statistics are staggering, including 16,726 rushing yards—an NFL record at the time that has been surpassed only once to this day—plus 110 rushing touchdowns and nine Pro Bowls. Payton was a Super Bowl champion, 1977 MVP, and a member of the Pro Football Hall of Fame and All-Decade Teams of the 1970s and 1980s. Off the field, Payton was equally impactful, known for his philanthropy and humanitarian efforts. He is so respected that the league named its most revered honor after him: the Walter Payton Man of the Year Award.

#20
NEW YORK GIANTS

- ⚔ **Frank Gifford** ⚔
- ⚔ **Lawrence Taylor** ⚔
- ⚔ **Michael Strahan** ⚔
- ⚔ **Eli Manning** ⚔

In 1925, a New York businessman named Tim Mara—who had been born into poverty on the Lower East Side of Manhattan—made an investment that would prove to be among the greatest in the history of sports. For the sum of $500, he founded a pro football franchise in New York, which was one of five to join the NFL that year. Today, it is the only one of those teams that remains, and stands as the fourth-oldest franchise in the league. The Giants experienced success in their earliest years, winning their first NFL championship in 1927, and then two more in 1934 and 1938 under the leadership of iconic head coach Steve Owen. Their next successful era would come two decades later, under Jim Lee Howell and assistant coach Vince Lombardi. Legendary players such as Frank Gifford and Sam Huff led this squad to the NFL championship game six times between 1956 and 1963, winning the title in 1956.

In 1979, the Giants had their next breakthrough—they drafted QB Phil Simms and hired George Young as GM.

Young would remain in that role until 1997, winning Executive of the Year five times, and was inducted into the Hall of Fame in 2020. Head coach Bill Parcells was hired in 1983, under whom the Giants became a force; led by stars such as Lawrence Taylor and Simms, they won Super Bowl titles in 1986 and 1990.

The twenty-first century brought further achievements, including another Super Bowl victory following the 2007 season, under coach Tom Coughlin and quarterback Eli Manning; the team's stunning upset of the undefeated Patriots in Super Bowl XLII is routinely described as one of the greatest games in NFL history. New York would add one more championship in 2011, defeating Tom Brady, Bill Belichick, and the Patriots once again in a thrilling rematch.

In every way aside from chronology, the Giants' history begins with Lawrence Taylor, considered by many (very much including me) the greatest defensive player of all time. LT revolutionized the linebacker position, amassing more than 140 sacks. His accolades include eight first-team All-Pro selections and three Defensive Player of the Year honors. Taylor won two Super Bowls with the Giants and remains the most recent defender to win league MVP (1986).

Gifford, who to later generations would be known mostly for his long broadcasting career, was first a highly productive and versatile running back and wide receiver for the Giants from 1952 to 1964. He earned numerous accolades, including eight Pro Bowl selections and the MVP award in 1956.

Michael Strahan is another star whose media career, in the mind of many fans, has eclipsed his greatness on the field. But make no mistake: Strahan was as feared a pass rusher as there was in the league during his era. Drafted in 1993, Strahan quickly became a dominant force, earning seven Pro Bowl selections and being named Defensive Player of the Year in 2001. He played a pivotal role in the Giants' Super Bowl XLII victory in his final game—sacking Tom Brady once—and was inducted into the Hall of Fame in 2014.

Rounding out the group is the quarterback who authored two of the greatest playoff runs of all time, forever cementing himself as a franchise legend. Eli Manning played sixteen seasons for the Giants, leading the Giants to two Super Bowl victories (XLII and XLVI), outdueling Tom Brady and earning Super Bowl MVP honors in both games. He was selected to four Pro Bowls and holds virtually every meaningful passing record in franchise history.

Despite the long droughts that have periodically afflicted their history, the Giants have stood as a towering colossus of the NFL, their storied legacy punctuated by thrilling victories, iconic players, and a resolute relevancy that has shaped the very fabric of football folklore, practically since its beginning.

#21
BOSTON RED SOX

⚔ **Ted Williams** ⚔
⚔ **Carl Yastrzemski** ⚔
⚔ **Pedro Martínez** ⚔
⚔ **David Ortiz** ⚔

The history of the Boston Red Sox has been like something out of a Charles Dickens novel: the best of times, and the worst of times. The highs have been as high as those of practically any franchise, while the worst was precipitated by the most infamous trade in sports history and led to a championship drought that lasted the better part of a century. The organization was founded in 1901 as one of the American League's eight charter franchises and was originally named the Boston Americans; they became the Red Sox in 1908, adopting the moniker to match their iconic red socks. The team's early years saw championships in 1903 and 1912, setting the table for Babe Ruth. Ruth's tenure included three more World Series titles until—in one of the most controversial transactions of all time—the Red Sox traded him to the Yankees in 1919, initiating the infamous "Curse of the Bambino," the championship drought that would haunt the team for decades.

The Red Sox were still competitive over the decades that followed, led by icons of the game such as Ted

Williams and Carl Yastrzemski. Boston would endure numerous near misses and heartbreaking defeats, including losses in the World Series in 1946, 1967, 1975, and 1986. They finally broke the curse in 2004, staging a historic comeback against their archrivals, the Yankees, in the ALCS, and then sweeping the Cardinals in the World Series, capturing their first championship in eighty-six years. Once that barrier was crossed, the Red Sox became one of the most successful teams of this century, winning three more titles over the following fourteen years. In all, the team has won nine World Series championships in its history; only the Yankees and Cardinals have won more.

Ted Williams is an easy choice for first face of the franchise; inarguably the greatest player in Boston history, and very much arguably as great a hitter as has ever lived. Williams played for the Red Sox from 1939 to 1960, though he missed nearly five seasons to serve as a pilot in two different wars. Williams boasted a career batting average of .344, with 521 home runs and 1,839 RBI, and remains the last player to hit over .400 in a single season (.406 in 1941). Williams earned two American League MVP awards and was inducted into the Baseball Hall of Fame in 1966.

Carl Yastrzemski played for the Red Sox from 1961 to 1983, winning the Triple Crown in 1967 after leading the league in batting average, home runs, and RBI. Yastrzemski was an eighteen-time all-star, won seven Gold Gloves, and was inducted into the Hall in 1989.

While Williams and Yaz were the most accomplished players the franchise ever produced, Pedro Martínez and David Ortiz are the forever faces of Boston's return to glory and the end of the dreaded curse. Martínez's tenure with the Red Sox was characterized by mind-boggling brilliance on the mound: over seven seasons in Boston, he amassed a 117–37 record, 2.52 ERA, and 1,683 strikeouts. He threw seven scoreless innings in winning Game 3 of the 2004 World Series in St. Louis, putting Boston on the precipice. Ortiz, meanwhile, played for the Red Sox from 2003 to 2016, hitting 483 home runs for the franchise. During the 2004 championship run, Ortiz played a pivotal role in the team's historic comeback against the Yankees in the ALCS, delivering multiple clutch hits, including walk-off heroics in Game 4 and Game 5. He would win MVP of that ALCS, a series that remains among the most dramatic in the history of the game.

A final element that favorably weights the franchise is the ballpark it calls home. Fenway Park is hallowed ground in baseball lore, unique among stadiums with its intimate dimensions and iconic features: The Green Monster, looming large in left field, challenging hitters and shaping strategy; the quirky dimensions, including the short distance down the line in right to the Pesky Pole, adding unpredictability to each game; the rich history, dating back to 1912. Fenway imbues every home game with a sense of tradition and nostalgia in which the spirit of baseball thrives.

#22
GOLDEN STATE WARRIORS

× **Wilt Chamberlain** ×
× **Rick Barry** ×
× **Stephen Curry** ×
× **Draymond Green** ×

In 1946, during pro basketball's infancy, the Philadelphia Warriors emerged as stalwarts of the fledgling Basketball Association of America (BAA), laying the foundation for a legacy of greatness. Led by Joe Fulks, they clinched the BAA championship in 1947. In 1956, they boasted the first "Big Three"—before there was such a thing—winning a title with Paul Arizin, Tom Gola, and Neil Johnston. In 1959, the Warriors added Wilt Chamberlain, who (despite never leading the franchise to a championship) put up some of the most legendary seasons in basketball history, including 1961–62, in which he averaged 50.4 points and 25.7 rebounds per game. The next golden era came in the Golden State: led by Rick Barry, the Warriors would claim another title in 1975, playing in Oakland. Of course, the most recent iteration of the Warriors has been a decade-long dynastic run, led by Stephen Curry, one of the best—and most beloved—players in NBA history. In the 2014–15 season, the dynamic duo of Curry and Klay Thompson blazed a trail of destruction, amassing a franchise-best 67–15 regular-season record. Their meteoric rise culminated in a thunderous crescendo as they clinched the championship, ending a forty-year title drought. In the following season, the Warriors shattered records with a 73–9 regular-season record, rewriting the narrative of basketball excellence. The addition of Kevin Durant would lead to two more championships and a third trip to the NBA Finals. After Durant's departure, the Warriors would win another championship in 2022, with Curry earning Finals MVP honors and cementing his legacy among the greatest to ever play.

Widely regarded as the greatest shooter of all time, Curry has fundamentally revolutionized the game, influencing teams—and aspiring players around the globe—to attempt more long-distance shots. He is a four-time champion and two-time MVP, with two scoring titles and ten All-NBA selections. With his unique blend of skill, finesse, and leadership, Curry has left an indelible mark on the game of basketball, inspiring generations of players to come.

Chamberlain's seasons with the Warriors, which encompass stints in Philadelphia and Northern California, are, without reasonable debate, the most dominant the game has ever seen. Over his six years for the franchise, he averaged 41.5 points and 25.1 rebounds in 47.2 minutes. Remarkably, he won only one of his four MVP awards during those years; it came in his rookie season of 1959–60, in which he was also named Rookie of the Year.

Rick Barry's first stint with the Warriors from 1965 to 1967 included a trip to the Finals in which they were beaten by Chamberlain's 76ers, despite Barry averaging 40.8 points in the series, a record that stood for three decades, only beaten by Michael Jordan in 1993. After multiple seasons with other teams, Barry would return and lead the Warriors to the title in 1975 in a sweep over Washington. In all, Barry averaged 25.6 points during his eight seasons with the Warriors, and his uniform number 24 was retired by the franchise in 1988.

The selection of Draymond Green over Klay Thompson and Steve Kerr, among others, was the result of hours of painstaking deliberation. In the end, Green was the most indispensable member of the quartet that has won four titles. At his size, his rebounding and playmaking prowess have changed the math for opponents—few players so big can facilitate the offense as he can, while even fewer so small can play the center position so effectively. Further, Green's fiery brand of leadership and rugged, physical style have been defining features of the Warriors' dynastic run.

#23
ATHLETICS

 ✕ **Connie Mack** ✕
 ✕ **Jimmie Foxx** ✕
 ✕ **Reggie Jackson** ✕
 ✕ **Rickey Henderson** ✕

Two decades of frustration on the field, coupled with regular embarrassing headlines about ballparks and local politics, have served to obscure one critically important fact about baseball's Athletics: For most of their history, they have been among the most successful franchises in the sport. Founded in Philadelphia in 1901 and located in Oakland from 1968 to 2024, the A's have won fifteen pennants and nine World Series titles.

In their earliest days, the A's were a dominant force led by some of the game's greatest stars, such as Eddie Collins, Jimmie Foxx, and Lefty Grove. Under manager Connie Mack, they won five championships between 1910 and 1930. In the early 1970s, under the leadership of owner Charlie Finley, the Swingin' A's won three consecutive World Series (1972–1974) behind the enormous bat of Reggie Jackson and the dominant arms of Catfish Hunter, Vida Blue, and Rollie Fingers. The next championship roster in Oakland featured the Bash Brothers, José Canseco and Mark McGwire, who led Tony LaRussa's team to three straight pennants and a championship in 1989. In later years, despite financial constraints, the A's showcased remarkable talent; the Moneyball era, spearheaded by general manager Billy Beane, brought notable success with an emphasis on analytics.

Only one name can begin the discussion for this franchise, and that is Cornelius McGillicuddy. Known as Connie Mack, his A's career spanned six decades, as a manager and team owner. Mack's managerial tenure with the Athletics from 1901 to 1950 remains unparalleled, as he holds the record for most wins by a manager by a significant margin. (Mack has 3,731 wins, 847 more than LaRussa, who is second all-time.) Mack also pioneered many aspects of modern baseball management, including platooning and scouting. He helped establish baseball's farm system and was instrumental in forming the American League.

Jimmie Foxx made his debut in 1925 at the age of seventeen, primarily as a first baseman, and played his first eleven seasons in Philadelphia, winning American League MVP awards in 1932 and 1933. Over those two seasons, Foxx combined to hit 106 home runs and drive in 332 runs.

Because the sport has always been tilted north and east, Reggie Jackson is today remembered more for his time with the Yankees; but the truth is, his longest tenure, and most of his best seasons, came in Oakland. Jackson, playing for the A's from 1967 to 1975 (and again in 1987), was named to six all-star games, won AL MVP in 1973, and was the signature star of the teams that won three straight championships—still the only franchise besides the Yankees ever to accomplish that feat.

Rickey Henderson, the best leadoff hitter in baseball history (when that was still a thing), played fourteen seasons in four different stints for the A's. Initially joining the team in 1979, he became their catalyst, revolutionizing the game with his power, unparalleled speed, and base-running acumen. Henderson won the AL MVP with Oakland in 1990 and hit .474 with three stolen bases in the A's sweep of their archrivals, the Giants, in the 1989 World Series. His number 24 was retired by the franchise in 2009.

#24
TORONTO MAPLE LEAFS

✕ **Turk Broda** ✕
✕ **Tim Horton** ✕
✕ **Darryl Sittler** ✕
✕ **Mats Sundin** ✕

There are few teams in the modern world of sports with histories more complicated than that of the Maple Leafs. Among the Original Six teams in the NHL, the Leafs saw enormous success in the league's first iteration. Under the leadership of legendary owner Conn Smythe, the Leafs won the Cup in 1932, then six times in the ten seasons spanning 1942–51, including a threepeat from 1947 to 1949 with legends such as Turk Broda, Ted Kennedy, Harry Watson, and Syl Apps. The 1960s brought more success, with the Leafs winning Stanley Cups in 1962, 1963, 1964, and 1967 on the backs of teams that featured Johnny Bower, Tim Horton, George Armstrong, and Frank Mahovlich.

In all, the Maple Leafs had won thirteen championships by the time of the NHL's expansion in 1967. That total was—and remains—the second most of any team, behind only the Canadiens. The trouble is the Leafs have not won a Stanley Cup since the NHL expanded beyond six teams; their drought of fifty-six seasons is the longest in league history. The rich history of a founding franchise with more Hall of Famers than any NHL team has been largely overshadowed; despite having one of the largest fan bases in all North American sports, most of its fans are too young to have ever seen the Leafs win the Cup.

Broda was Toronto's first megastar, playing 629 games over fourteen seasons and winning the Stanley Cup five times. Broda was legendary for his calm demeanor under pressure, which was never more on display than in 1942, when he led the Leafs to a Stanley Cup victory after being down 3–0 in the Final to the Red Wings. Broda was inducted into the Hall of Fame in 1967.

The founder of the iconic coffee-and-donut shops that bear his name, defenseman Tim Horton played twenty seasons for the Maple Leafs, winning four Stanley Cups. Horton appeared in 486 consecutive regular-season games, which remains the Leafs record (and was the NHL record for consecutive games by a defenseman until 2007). Universally acknowledged as the strongest man in the league during his time, Horton was still an active NHL player—with the Buffalo Sabres—when he was killed in an auto accident at the age of forty-four. In 2016, more than four decades after his death, Horton's number 7 was retired by the Maple Leafs.

Darryl Sittler spent the majority of his fifteen-year career with Toronto, serving as their captain beginning in 1975, the same year he became the first player in franchise history with 100 points in a season. In February 1976, Sittler set an NHL record (that still stands) with six goals and four assists for ten points in a game against Boston. He remains the last player to score six goals in a single game. Sittler was elected to the Hall of Fame in 1989 and named one of the 100 greatest players in NHL history in 2017.

Rounding out the foursome is Mats Sundin, the Swedish center who played thirteen seasons with the Maple Leafs from 1994 to 2008, serving as captain for over a decade. He holds the franchise records for career goals (420) and points (987) and was the team's leading scorer in twelve of his thirteen seasons in Toronto. Sundin averaged a point per game with Toronto, totaling 987 points in 981 regular-season games and 70 more in 77 play-off games.

#25
PHILADELPHIA 76ERS

× **Dolph Schayes** ×
× **Julius Erving** ×
× **Allen Iverson** ×
× **Joel Embiid** ×

I f you are an astute fan, you may be aware that the Sixers, as we've known them since 1963, were founded as the Syracuse Nationals in 1946. What you likely do not know is that the original owner, Danny Biasone, is credited with one of the most significant rule changes in basketball history. In 1954, with the NBA facing such financial struggles that there were only eight teams operating, Biasone suggested installing a shot clock to increase the action and make the game more enjoyable for fans. He developed a twenty-four-second timer, which would prompt at least thirty shots per quarter. The shot clock was an immediate hit, and the rest is history.

Upon moving to Philadelphia in 1963, the Sixers soon became a dominant force behind the brilliance of Wilt Chamberlain, who led the team to a 68–13 record and the franchise's second championship in 1966–67; Chamberlain averaged over 24 points and 24 rebounds on the season.

The 76ers emerged as contenders again in the 1980s,

led by Julius Erving and later by Moses Malone; they reached the NBA Finals three times from 1980 to 1983, winning their third championship in 1983 with Malone named Finals MVP. I have always maintained that—for that one season—those Sixers were the best team I ever saw; they dropped just one playoff game on their way to that title, after Malone offered the legendary prediction of "Fo', Fo', Fo'."

The 76ers have not won the championship since that year. In fact, they would not return to the Finals until the 2000–01 season, led by league MVP Allen Iverson, and have not been back since. More recent efforts have been defined by postseason disappointment despite star-caliber players, including Joel Embiid.

Had Malone played longer than five years for Philadelphia, he'd have been an easy choice here—instead, his teammate Erving is the first face of the franchise. Playing for the Sixers from 1976 to 1987, Dr. J led the Sixers to the Finals four times, winning it all in 1983. He was an eleven-time NBA all-star (all eleven with the 76ers), five-time All-NBA First Team, and, even more importantly, his spectacular grace and athleticism transformed the game, paving the way for high-flying superstars such as Michael Jordan.

Iverson is an equally easy choice; like Erving, he was a lot of people's favorite player, and inspired a generation of hoopers with his fearlessness, style, and unstoppable crossover dribble. He won league MVP in 2001 and the scoring title four times in the seven seasons spanning 1999–2005; his jersey number 3 was retired by the Sixers in 2014.

While not as well remembered as some other stars of the league's earliest days, Dolph Schayes was a twelve-time All-NBA selection, playing his entire career for the Nationals and then the Sixers. During his fifteen seasons, he led his team to the playoffs fourteen times (including the title in 1955). He finished his career as a player-coach, then coached two more seasons after his playing days, winning Coach of the Year in 1966. He was named to the NBA's 50 Greatest Players list and the league's 75th Anniversary team, as well as being inducted into the Hall of Fame in 1973.

Joel Embiid earns the final spot ahead of Hal Greer and Charles Barkley as much for the hope he brings as the success he's enjoyed. While Barkley played just eight seasons in Philadelphia, Embiid's injury-plagued roller-coaster ride began with Philly drafting him third overall in 2014 out of Kansas. At his apex, he has been as effective as any player in the NBA, winning the MVP in 2023 and making five All-NBA teams. Embiid is undoubtedly the face of the modern franchise, and if the Sixers return to the mountaintop any time in the foreseeable future, it will surely be because he led the way.

#26
CINCINNATI REDS

- ✖ **Pete Rose** ✖
- ✖ **Johnny Bench** ✖
- ✖ **Joe Morgan** ✖
- ✖ **Barry Larkin** ✖

The Cincinnati Reds, as we have known them for well over a century, exist because of a newspaperman who liked beer. The original Reds formed in 1876 as one of the charter members of the National League, but were expelled in 1880 after refusing to sign a pledge disallowing beer sale at home games. O. P. Caylor, baseball columnist at the *Cincinnati Enquirer,* was so enraged at this outcome that he led a group that formed a new team (initially called the Red Stockings), and a new league called the American Association. Seven years later, the Red Stockings shortened their name to Reds, and they joined the National League in 1890.

The franchise won its first World Series in 1919, though the victory was soon overshadowed by evidence that their opponents—the notorious Black Sox—had thrown the series. Cincinnati would be the scene of several other "firsts" in the 1930s, including MLB's first night game (1935), the first fireworks night (on that same night), and pitcher Johnny Vander Meer becoming the first (and still only) pitcher to throw back-to-back no-hitters, in 1938.

The greatest era in franchise history came in the 1970s, with the dynasty known as the Big Red Machine. They won back-to-back World Series in 1975 and 1976, led by superstars Pete Rose (425 hits in 1975–76), Johnny Bench (184 RBI in 1975–76), and Joe Morgan (National League MVP in 1975 and 1976). The Reds would win four pennants ('70, '72, '75, '76), with an MLB-best .592 winning percentage across the decade.

Rose, Bench, and Morgan are easy choices for this list, as the most prominent faces of one of the most memorable dynasties of the modern era. More difficult, by far, is excluding other stars of the Big Red Machine, including Hall of Famer Tony Perez, who earned seven all-star selections in sixteen seasons with Cincinnati, and manager Sparky Anderson, who won four pennants in his nine seasons. However, the inclusion of either of them would mean the exclusion of Barry Larkin, who played his entire nineteen-year career in Cincinnati, earning twelve all-star selections and winning the NL MVP in 1995. Larkin's prowess at shortstop earned him three Gold Gloves to go with his career .295 batting average, 2,340 hits, and 379 stolen bases. Larkin's crowning achievement came in 1990 when he helped the Reds secure what remains their most recent World Series championship.

Finally, it should be noted that one of the sports' grandest traditions is the opening day parade in Cincinnati, which remains a highlight despite the recent changes in early-season scheduling across MLB. The Reds have started every season in Cincinnati since 1876, except for 1877, 1885, and 1966 because of rain, 1990 for a baseball lockout, and 1888, the only time the team was scheduled to start on the road.

#27
NEW YORK ISLANDERS

✗ **Billy Smith** ✗
✗ **Denis Potvin** ✗
✗ **Bryan Trottier** ✗
✗ **Mike Bossy** ✗

I n the four leagues that have traditionally constituted the major sports in North America, there are only four franchises that have won four consecutive championships. The first to accomplish the feat was the Yankees, from 1936 to 1939, led by legends such as Lou Gehrig and Joe DiMaggio. The franchise would again string together five in a row a generation later, from 1949 to 1953. Later in that decade, the Canadiens would win five consecutive Stanley Cups, from 1956 to 1960, a feat the franchise would nearly match with four straight from 1976 to 1979. The Celtics, possessors of the longest dynasty in American professional sports, won eight consecutive NBA championships from 1959 to 1966. What these three runs have in common is that they were all performed by foundational franchises of their respective sports, teams with long and rich histories and traditions of success—these three franchises have won a combined seventy championships.

This history serves to make the New York Islanders' dynasty of the 1980s feel even more improbable; it was the unlikeliest all-time great run our sports nation has ever witnessed. The Islanders did not begin play until 1972–73. While they struggled in their debut season, they quickly began to build a competitive roster, with their first break-through coming in 1975, when they reached the playoffs for the first time. The Islanders' golden era began in the early 1980s, marked by four consecutive Stanley Cup championships from 1980 to 1983. This dynasty boasted a formidable lineup, including Hall of Famers Mike Bossy, Bryan Trottier, Denis Potvin, and Billy Smith.

In the 1981–82 season, the Islanders set a franchise record with 118 points, winning the Prince of Wales Trophy for the first of three straight seasons. For a time, they also held the record for the longest win streak—fifteen games without a loss—in NHL history. In all, the Islanders won nineteen consecutive playoff series, a feat that remains unparalleled in NHL history, and remain the authors of the last professional "four-peat" in any of the four sports leagues covered in this book. (Though it should be noted the Houston Comets won the first four WNBA titles from 1997 to 2000, only for the franchise to be disbanded in 2008.)

All four faces for the Islanders franchise hail from the golden era, fittingly one for each of the four Stanley Cup titles. If there were space for a fifth, it would no doubt belong to Al Arbour, who coached the Islanders to all four of their championships and remains the only man to ever coach 1,500 games for the same team. Meanwhile, the rivalry between the Islanders and the Rangers was, during those dynasty years and to this day, one of the fiercest in all of sports. There is no doubt that Rangers fans will take exception with this selection of the Isles ahead of the Original Six franchise in the heart of New York City. However, the choice is neither complicated nor controversial: The two franchises have won the exact same number of championships, despite the Rangers having a more than four-decades–long head start. The Rangers have a rich tradition and an infinitely larger fan base, but based on their golden era, the Islanders deserve this place above them in the standings of history.

#28
MIAMI HEAT

⚔ Pat Riley ⚔
⚔ Alonzo Mourning ⚔
⚔ Dwyane Wade ⚔
⚔ LeBron James ⚔

Since its inception, the NBA has been defined by the Celtics and the Lakers. No reasonable fan would ever argue otherwise. However, you might be surprised to learn that the third best winning percentage in playoff history belongs to the Miami Heat. In fact, in their comparatively short history, the Heat have been as consistently success-ful as any franchise. Miami has made the playoffs in 69 percent of its seasons; by contrast, the Bulls have qualified for the postseason in 62 percent of their seasons, while the Warriors have made it in only 47 percent of theirs.

The Heat were founded in 1988, with a name inspired by Miami's reputation as a hub of sunshine and energy; but, in many ways, the franchise was really born in 1995, when Pat Riley was given control to mold it as he saw fit. The winning began almost immediately and has hardly ceased since. Led by the dynamic duo of Dwyane Wade and Shaquille O'Neal, the Heat won their first champion-ship in 2006, defeating Dallas in six games, with Wade earning Finals MVP honors.

In the summer of 2010, Miami transformed the entire sport with their acquisitions of LeBron James and Chris Bosh, forming the most famous (or infamous) Big Three in basketball history. They would reach the Finals in all four seasons James played in Miami, winning the first two rings of James's career. The Heat did not crater after LeBron's departure: They've not won fewer than thirty-seven games in any season since he left, they've made the playoffs in seven of ten seasons, and they've reached the Finals twice. Led by Riley and his outstanding protégé Erik Spoelstra, "Heat Culture" has come to stand for old-school toughness and grit—in many ways a throwback to how the sport used to feel, but rarely does anymore.

Riley, one of the most recognizable faces in the history of basketball, is the first face in Miami for certain. High-level winning followed him from Los Angeles to New York to South Florida and never stopped. He has led a franchise that had never won a playoff series to three championships and seven Finals appearances. His fingerprints have been all over every aspect of the franchise and Heat Culture, including the acquisitions of its three other faces, as well as Spoelstra, who was one of the more painful omissions of this entire exercise.

Wade is the greatest player in Heat history on the court, and the most important off the basketball floor. Along with Riley, Wade made basketball cool in sweltering South Florida. Despite playing with such celebrated legends as

O'Neal and James, the Heat always remained Wade's team. He ranks as the team's all-time leader in points, assists, steals, and games played, earning thirteen all-star selections and the 2006 Finals MVP award.

LeBron James taking his talents to South Beach stands as one of the most memorable and significant events in basketball history. While he played only four years for the Heat, they stand as four of the greatest seasons any player has ever had. He finished top three in league MVP voting in all four seasons, winning the award twice. He led the Heat to the Finals in all four, winning two rings and being named Finals MVP both times.

During Alonzo Mourning's tenure with the Heat from 1995 to 2002, and again from 2005 to 2008, he became a cornerstone of the franchise, earning two Defensive Player of the Year awards. He ranks as the franchise's all-time leader in blocks, second all-time leader in rebounds, and third in games played.

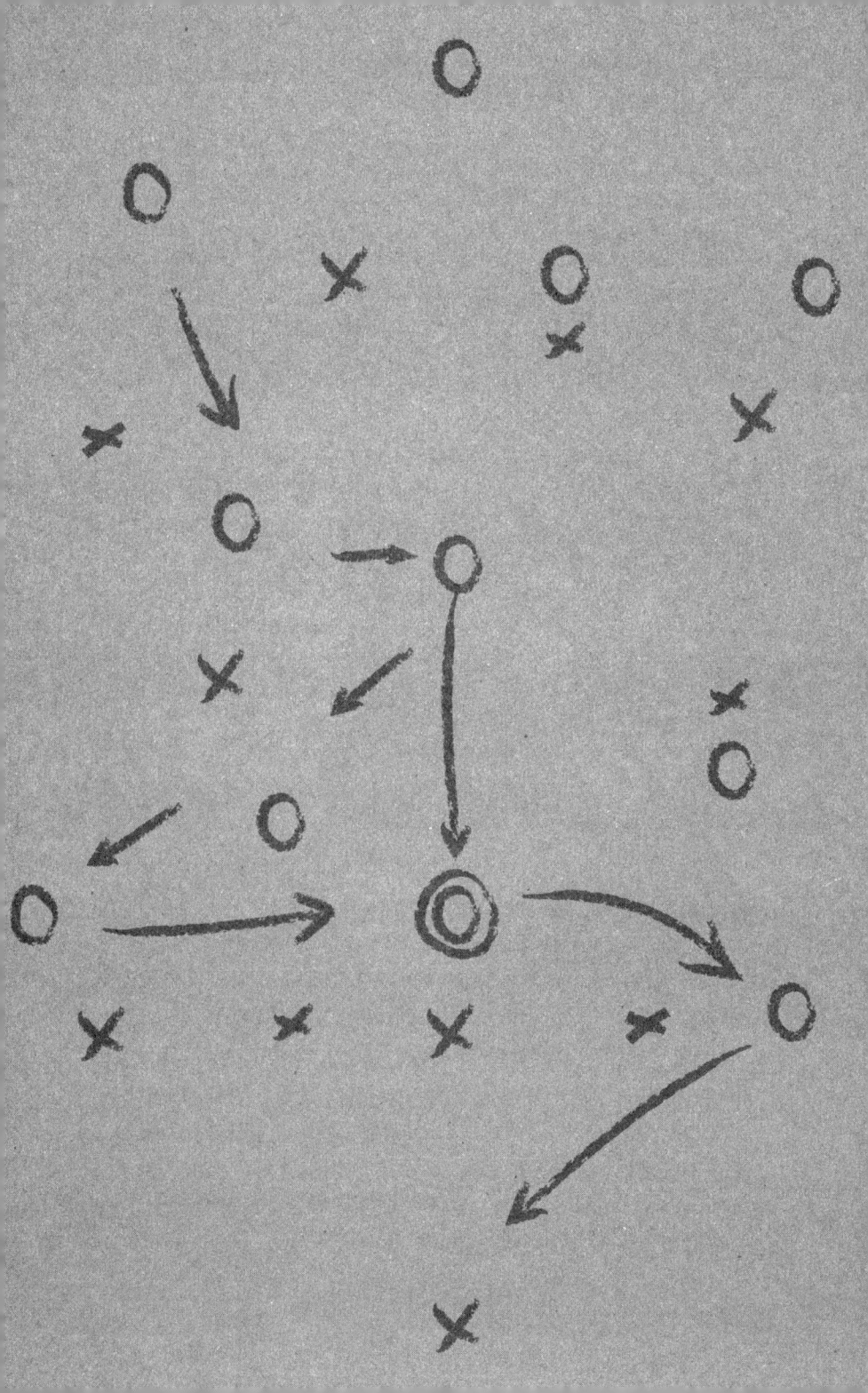

THE
THRILLING
THIRTY-TWO

—

We know that hockey is where we live, where we can best meet and overcome pain and wrong and death. Life is just a place where we spend time between games.

—Fred Shero, Philadelphia Flyers

#29
CLEVELAND BROWNS

× **Paul Brown** ×
× **Otto Graham** ×
× **Jim Brown** ×
× **Joe Thomas** ×

Among the many unfortunate by-products of the decades of misery endured by the Browns and their faithful is that there are now multiple generations of football fans who have no idea that at one point in time this franchise represented the very best of pro football. The Browns once set a standard most other teams could only imagine, and created a brand that resonated like practically no other. The franchise was cofounded in 1944 by its original coach, Paul Brown, whose name belongs on the short list of the greatest in the history of the sport. They were a charter member of the short-lived All-America Football Conference, which lasted four seasons, with the Browns winning the conference's championship in each of its four years. The Browns—along with the Baltimore Colts and San Francisco 49ers—joined the NFL when the AAFC folded, and proceeded to win the NFL championship in their very first season. They would win again in 1954, 1955, and 1964, along the way qualifying for the league championship game in each of their first six NFL seasons. Thus, in the first ten years of their existence, the Browns played for the championship every single season.

If you find all this surprising, it is because since the 1970s, the Browns have been known more for causing their legendary fans all manner of heartbreak: from excruciating postseason losses to the franchise's infamous relocation to Baltimore, and, most recently, two decades of mostly terrible teams after their reinstatement in Cleveland in 1999. The Browns did not post a single winning season in the 2010s, and in 2017 became only the second team ever to post an 0–16 record. They are one of four active NFL teams never to appear in a Super Bowl.

The team was named for its first coach, and Paul Brown will always be its first face. Too often overlooked when the game's great coaches are listed, Brown was unpopular with his players due to his famously rigid style, but there is no arguing the results: In seventeen seasons in Cleveland, his teams went 158–48–8 and won seven championships. (Brown also won a collegiate national championship at Ohio State, becoming the first coach ever to win championships at the pro and college levels of football, and the only one until Jimmy Johnson joined him some four decades later.)

Brown's quarterback for all seven of his pro championships was Otto Graham, the most prolific passer of the game's early days. Graham was named MVP three times in the NFL and twice in the AAFC. His record as starting quarterback in the NFL was 57–13–1, including a 9–3 mark in the playoffs; he continues to hold the record for the highest career win percentage by a starting quarterback.

Ironically, not only was Graham not the greatest player in franchise history, but Paul Brown was also not even the greatest Cleveland "Brown" of all time. Those honors are held by Jim Brown, and figure to be for a very long time. Brown played just nine seasons in the NFL, retiring at the age of thirty, and departed as the league's record holder for single-season (1,863 in 1963) and career rushing yards (12,312), as well as top of the all-time lists in rushing touchdowns (106), total touchdowns (126), and all-purpose yards (15,549). There are many who will argue that Brown was the single greatest player ever to wear an NFL uniform, and those people will hear no argument from me.

The final face of this franchise belongs to Joe Thomas, who had the bad fortune of playing nearly his entire career during the dark ages of Cleveland football. Thomas, a constant bright spot in his eleven seasons with the Browns, was an All-Pro eight times and was selected to ten Pro Bowls. He holds the NFL record for most consecutive snaps at 10,363 and was a first ballot inductee into the Pro Football Hall of Fame in 2023.

30

CHICAGO BLACKHAWKS

- ✕ **Bobby Hull** ✕
- ✕ **Stan Mikita** ✕
- ✕ **Patrick Kane** ✕
- ✕ **Jonathan Toews** ✕

The origin of the name of the NHL franchise awarded to Chicago in 1926 is likely not what you expect: Owner Frederic McLaughlin had been a commander with the 333rd Machine Gun Battalion during World War I, in an infantry unit nicknamed the Blackhawk Division. Thus began the storied history of the NHL's then-westernmost franchise, which would win two Stanley Cups in the 1930s, one in the 1960s, and then three in an impressive six-season span in the 2010s.

Those long decades of failure between Stanley Cups were the result of a frustrating (or, incomprehensible) ownership situation. After the death of McLaughlin, the team was sold to a syndicate headed by longtime team president Bill Tobin, who proved to be a lackey for James Norris, who owned the archrival Red Wings. As a result of this relationship, ownership paid almost no attention to the Chicago team for nearly a decade, with many trades orchestrated between the teams intended to bolster Detroit. The rebirth of the Chicago franchise in the 1960s was led by new owners, Arthur Wirtz and his son, Bill Wirtz, and by the team's greatest star, Bobby Hull. They would reach the Stanley Cup Final three times in the decade, winning in 1961, the only championship the franchise would celebrate between 1938 and 2010.

Known as the Golden Jet, Hull is the first face of the Blackhawks, scoring 604 goals during his time in Chicago, making him the franchise's all-time leading goal scorer. He won three Art Ross Trophies as the league's leading scorer and two Hart Memorial Trophies as the NHL's most valuable player.

In 2011, the franchise erected statues outside their arena that honored Hull and his longtime teammate Stan Mikita, whose tenure with the Blackhawks spanned from 1958 to 1980. Renowned for his exceptional playmaking, Mikita amassed 1,467 points in 1,396 games, making him the franchise's all-time leading point scorer. He claimed four Art Ross Trophies as the league's top point scorer and two Hart Memorial Trophies as MVP—plus his sportsmanship was recognized with two Lady Byng Memorial Trophies for gentlemanly conduct.

The renaissance of Chicago hockey provides the final faces, beginning with Patrick Kane, who made his debut in 2007. Kane amassed 1,225 points in Chicago, making him one of the franchise's all-time leading scorers, and played a pivotal role in the team's Stanley Cup victories in 2010, 2013, and 2015, earning the Conn Smythe Trophy as the playoff MVP in 2013. Kane has consistently been among the league's top scorers, winning the Art Ross Trophy in 2016 with 106 points.

Jonathan Toews also arrived in 2007 and quickly established himself as the team's leader. Toews captained the three Stanley Cup teams and starred with his signature two-way play; with over 800 career points, he is among the franchise's top scorers. His defensive prowess earned him the Frank J. Selke Trophy as the league's best defensive forward in 2013.

#31
KANSAS CITY CHIEFS

⚔ **Len Dawson** ⚔
⚔ **Derrick Thomas** ⚔
⚔ **Travis Kelce** ⚔
⚔ **Patrick Mahomes** ⚔

L amar Hunt, the son of an oil tycoon who was one of the richest individual people in the United States, was raised in Dallas and developed a great passion for sports; during his life, he would be enshrined in the National Soccer Hall of Fame, having been a founder of MLS, and the International Tennis Hall of Fame. (So significant was his contribution to soccer in this country, in fact, that the oldest ongoing national soccer tournament, the US Open Cup, now bears his name.) But it is his place in the Pro Football Hall of Fame for which he is best remembered. Hunt applied to the NFL in 1959 to bring an expansion franchise to Dallas and was turned down. In response, Hunt would spearhead a group of businessmen who formed the American Football League, and the Dallas Texans were a founding franchise.

In 1963, the team moved to Kansas City and was renamed the Chiefs, and practically from its very origin was highly successful: Under the leadership of Hall of Fame coach Hank Stram, the Chiefs won three AFL

Championships, and represented the league in two of the four Super Bowls before the AFL-NFL merger. The following decades saw the Chiefs fielding mostly competitive teams, which largely specialized in postseason disappointment; in one stretch from 1994 through 2017, they would lose ten of their eleven playoff games. The fortunes in Kansas City would change dramatically under coach Andy Reid with the selection of quarterback Patrick Mahomes in the 2017 draft. It is not too early to suggest that Mahomes is already among the greatest players in the history of the sport and is trending toward possibly being the greatest quarterback of all time. As of this writing, he and Reid have reached five Super Bowls together and have won three. In fact, he is one of only three players to win multiple regular-season MVPs and multiple Super Bowl MVPs, the others being Tom Brady and Joe Montana.

Both Mahomes and his favorite target, Travis Kelce, are obvious selections for this list. Kelce is fourth on the all-time receiving yards list for tight ends and has been the primary weapon on all three Kansas City championship teams of this era, while the three tight ends ahead of him (Tony Gonzalez, Jason Witten, and Antonio Gates) combined to win zero Super Bowls in their brilliant careers. Kelce is also the all-time leader in postseason receptions and Super Bowl receptions, at any position, and has amassed the second-most receiving yards and receiving touchdowns in playoff history, trailing only Jerry Rice in both categories.

Len Dawson was the original Chiefs legend, enjoying a storied career and fourteen seasons with the franchise, leading the league in completion percentage seven times and in touchdown passes four times. He was the MVP of Super Bowl IV and the all-time AFL leader in touchdowns passes (182), and was named to the second-team All-Time AFL roster, behind Joe Namath.

The final space here belongs to Derrick Thomas, who amassed 126.5 sacks over eleven seasons, averaging 11.5 sacks per season. Thomas added 41 forced fumbles in his career and set an NFL record with seven sacks in a single game (November 11, 1990). Named to nine Pro Bowls, he was the NFL Defensive Player of the Year runner-up in 1990. Inducted into the Pro Football Hall of Fame posthumously in 2009, he died at thirty-three after complications stemming from a car crash.

#32
PITTSBURGH PIRATES

* ✗ **Honus Wagner** ✗
* ✗ **Roberto Clemente** ✗
* ✗ **Bill Mazeroski** ✗
* ✗ **Willie Stargell** ✗

The year is 1876, the United States is celebrating its centennial, Alexander Graham Bell completes the first ever telephone call, Colorado becomes the thirty-eighth state in the union, and Heinz Ketchup, originally sold as "catsup," is first introduced to the world. In that year, in the city that today is home to Heinz Field, professional baseball was first played by a team called the Alleghenys, which joined the National League in 1887 and changed its name to the Pirates in 1895. More than three decades before the founding of the Steelers, and nearly eighty years before the Penguins, the Pirates represented the city at a junction of three rivers in western Pennsylvania.

The team found success in the early 1900s under manager Fred Clarke, winning their first World Series in 1909 behind the legendary play of Honus Wagner, who had eight hits and six stolen bases in the series. The Pirates' golden era came in the late 1960s and 1970s, ending with the "We Are Family" team of 1979, and boasted a roster filled with future Hall of Famers, including Roberto Clemente, Bill Mazeroski, Willie Stargell, and Dave Parker. In 1960, Mazeroski forever etched his name in baseball history by hitting a walk-off home run in Game 7 of the World Series against the Yankees, securing the Pirates' first championship since 1925.

Chronologically, Wagner is the first face of Pittsburgh sports, one of baseball's greatest shortstops of all time. Between 1900 to 1917, he won eight NL batting titles and led the Pirates to their first World Series championship in 1909.

Clemente, a fifteen-time all-star and twelve-time Gold Glove winner, remains the franchise's most beloved player. His legacy extends well beyond the field; a humanitarian, Clemente tragically died in a plane crash while delivering aid to earthquake victims in Nicaragua in 1972. Clemente's tenure, from 1955 to 1972, was marked by exceptional talent as well as his charity work. He amassed a .317 batting average, 240 home runs, and 1,305 RBI in 2,433 games, and, in what proved to be the final regular season at-bat of his career, making history as the first Latin American player to reach 3,000 hits.

Mazeroski was Clemente's teammate for that final game; they were the last two Pirates who had been on the 1960 championship team. While Maz will always be remembered for the home run that beat the Yankees, he was a defensive stalwart from 1956 to 1972, earning eight

Gold Gloves, and was inducted into the Hall of Fame in 2001.

Known as Pops, Stargell hit 475 home runs for Pittsburgh, a franchise record. His powerful bat made him a seven-time all-star, and he led the Pirates to two World Series titles, including in 1979 when he won the World Series MVP and hit 32 home runs.

#33
NEW YORK RANGERS

× **Rod Gilbert** ×
× **Brian Leetch** ×
× **Mark Messier** ×
× **Henrik Lundqvist** ×

F ounded in 1926, the New York Rangers, named after the Tex Rickard–led group that first brought hockey to Madison Square Garden, are one of the Original Six teams in the NHL. In their second season, they captured the Stanley Cup, setting a precedent for excellence that they would, unfortunately, struggle to sustain over the course of their history. The Rangers' earliest years were far and away their best, capturing three Stanley Cups in the years between their inception and 1940. However, it would be fifty-four years before they would raise the Cup again, and, despite good seasons and several near misses, they have not done it again since. Thus, this beloved franchise with as devoted a fan base as any in sports has won only one championship in the last eighty-five years.

Still, the Rangers have produced numerous Hall of Famers and iconic moments: from the Goal-a-Game line of the late 1960s and early '70s to "the Guarantee," where Mark Messier famously promised victory in a must-win game in the 1994 playoffs. Despite playing only ten of his twenty-five professional seasons in New York, Messier deserves his place on this list for delivering the only triumph generations of fans ever lived to see, tallying 30 points in 23 games in the 1994 postseason. The championship also made Messier the only player in NHL history to captain two different franchises to a Stanley Cup.

Rod Gilbert's career with the Rangers spanned from 1960 to 1978, totaling 1,021 points in 1,065 games—but his impact extended well beyond statistics as he became a beloved figure in Rangers lore, epitomizing skill, dedication, and leadership on the ice.

Defenseman Brian Leetch played seventeen seasons with the Rangers, totaling 981 points over 1,129 games. Leetch was a two-time Norris Trophy winner as the league's best defenseman, and his leadership was crucial in the Rangers' 1994 Stanley Cup, where he notched 34 points in 23 playoff games, earning the Conn Smythe Trophy.

Henrik Lundqvist is the face of the modern era of Rangers hockey, leading New York to twelve playoff appearances in fifteen years, including a memorable Stanley Cup Final run in 2014. King Henrik won the Vezina in 2012 and is the only goaltender in NHL history to record eleven thirty-win seasons in his first twelve seasons (and his twenty-four wins in 2012–13 led the NHL in a shortened season). He also holds the record for most career wins by a European-born goaltender in the NHL. Lundqvist's number 30 was retired by the Rangers in 2022.

#34
ATLANTA BRAVES

✳ **Warren Spahn** ✳
✳ **Hank Aaron** ✳
✳ **Greg Maddux** ✳
✳ **Chipper Jones** ✳

The history of the Atlanta Braves franchise, founded in 1871 as the Boston Red Stockings, features legendary names and some of the most famous moments baseball has ever produced—but has also been notable for their minimal high-level winning. The franchise has been around for more than 150 years and has made almost as many major changes in location as it has had championship seasons. The Braves began in Boston, moved to Milwaukee in 1953, and then to Atlanta in 1966. Three cities and just four World Series titles (1914, 1957, 1995, and 2021).

The most notable era for the Braves was during the 1990s and early 2000s, led by manager Bobby Cox and featuring a powerhouse pitching rotation dubbed the Big Three consisting of Greg Maddux, Tom Glavine, and John Smoltz. Atlanta dominated the National League East, winning an unprecedented fourteen consecutive division titles from 1991 to 2005. However, only one of those seasons resulted in a World Series championship, which came after a lockout-shortened campaign when the schedule was condensed to 144 games; fan enthusiasm was at an all-time low due to the prolonged labor strife, which had caused the cancellation of the World Series the year before.

Without close competition, the most iconic moment in franchise history was authored by Henry Aaron, who spent nearly all of his career with the Braves, and famously broke Babe Ruth's all-time home run record on April 8, 1974, while wearing a Braves uniform. Hammerin' Hank played twenty-one seasons for the Braves, and arguably his best in 1957 when he won the NL MVP with a major league–leading 44 home runs, 132 RBI, and 369 total bases. In all, he would hit 733 of his then-record 755 home runs for the Braves.

Warren Spahn spent twenty seasons with the franchise, earning all-star honors in fourteen of them. He would win 356 games for the Braves, with his best seasons coming in the 1950s; in 1953, Spahn posted a 23–7 record with an MLB-best 2.10 ERA. In 1957, he won the NL Cy Young award, leading the majors with 21 wins and 18 complete games. Spahn remains legendary for his consistency—he notched thirteen seasons with at least 20 wins—and his longevity, throwing his two career no-hitters in 1960 and 1961 at the ages of thirty-nine and forty.

Chipper Jones played his entire nineteen-season

career for the Braves and remains among the most beloved figures in the history of Atlanta sports. He would earn eight all-star selections, a batting title in 2008, and the 1999 NL MVP. Jones retired with 468 home runs, a .303 lifetime batting average, and a reputation as one of the greatest switch-hitters in baseball history.

Greg Maddux was a pitching maestro, excelling with precision and finesse. Among his highlights during his eleven seasons in Atlanta were three of his four consecutive Cy Young Awards, and ten of his eighteen Gold Gloves. Among his most notable statistics—of which there are far too many to list—my favorite is this: In 1997, Maddux issued a total of twenty walks in 232.2 innings pitched.

#35
DETROIT TIGERS

× **Ty Cobb** ×
× **Hank Greenberg** ×
× **Al Kaline** ×
× **Miguel Cabrera** ×

What we know today as baseball's American League was formed in 1894 as the Western League, which operated until it was renamed in 1900 as a competitor to the National League. The Western League was composed of eight charter franchises; the Tigers are the only one still in their original home. The history of the Tigers has been filled with peaks and valleys—highlighted by some of the game's most enduring stars leading the way to championships across various generations. Their earliest years were built around the brilliance of Ty Cobb, who spent twenty-two seasons with the Tigers and became the greatest star of his era. The Tigers would win their first World Series in 1935, win it again in 1945, led by Hank Greenberg, and win another in 1968, a season in which pitcher Denny McLain won thirty-one games. Alan Trammell and Lou Whitaker formed a dynamic duo in the infield during the 1980s, bringing the city its most recent championship in 1984. After another lengthy drought, it was Justin Verlander's dominance on the mound that brought the Tigers back to the World Series in 2006 and 2012; in all, the Tigers have won four World Series and eleven pennants.

Cobb, known as the Georgia Peach, is the first face of the franchise, chronologically and in every other way as well. Playing twenty-two of his twenty-four seasons in Detroit, Cobb owns the highest career batting average in AL history at .367, having amassed 4,191 official hits, a record that stood for more than half a century after his retirement. Cobb won twelve batting titles throughout his career, dominating the sport with his aggressive play. Despite a legacy tarnished by allegations of violence and racism, Cobb received the highest percentage of votes for the Hall of Fame of any player until Tom Seaver in 1992.

Hank Greenberg was born in New York and was courted by the Yankees, but because Lou Gehrig was entrenched at first base, Greenberg found his way to Detroit, where he played twelve seasons. Among the greatest right-handed hitters of all time, Greenberg's notable statistics include hitting 58 home runs in 1938, just two shy of Babe Ruth's single-season record, and leading the league in RBI in four different seasons (including 184 in 1937). He won two American League MVP awards and was a five-time all-star, despite missing three full seasons and parts of two others to serve in World War II; he was the first major leaguer to join the armed forces and spent forty-seven months in the military, the longest stint of any player, all during what would have been the prime of his career.

To this day, there may be no figure more associated with the franchise than Al Kaline, known as Mr. Tiger, who played twenty-two seasons in Detroit, and was then featured on the team's broadcasts from his retirement in 1975 through 2002. Kaline then moved into the front office, where he remained until his death in 2020; in all, Al Kaline was associated with the Tigers for sixty-seven years. A fifteen-time all-star, he earned ten Gold Gloves for his exceptional outfield defense and collected 3,007 hits along with 399 home runs.

Miguel Cabrera played sixteen seasons in Detroit, establishing himself among the most consistent hitters of all time. The highlight of his career came in 2012, as Cabrera led the Tigers to the pennant, becoming the first hitter in forty-five seasons to win the Triple Crown, hitting .330 with 44 home runs and 139 RBI. A recitation of all Cabrera's offensive statistics would require pages to do justice, but my favorite among them is this: In the history of the sport there are only three players with 500 home runs, 3,000 hits, and a career average above .300—Henry Aaron, Willie Mays, and Miguel Cabrera.

#36
COLORADO AVALANCHE

× **Peter Šťastný** ×
× **Joe Sakic** ×
× **Peter Forsberg** ×
× **Patrick Roy** ×

The Quebec Nordiques were among the founding franchises of the World Hockey Association in 1972, and then one of the four that merged into the NHL seven years later. While they never won the Stanley Cup, the Nordiques were generally a good team through most of the 1980s, qualifying for the playoffs in seven consecutive seasons from 1981 to 1987. A significant decline would soon follow, however, beginning in 1988—Quebec finished last in its division in five consecutive seasons, two of which saw them post the worst record in the NHL, including an unsightly twelve-win season in 1990. The franchise's on-ice issues, though, paled in comparison to the financial challenges; Quebec City was, by a wide margin, the smallest market in the NHL. By 1995, the franchise had relocated to Denver, and instantly found enormous success, winning the Stanley Cup in their first season in Colorado and again five years after that. That first championship in 1996 made the Avalanche the first Denver-based team in the four major sports leagues to win a league title.

Before there was an Avalanche, there was Peter Šťastný, the greatest star of the team's Quebec era and the second-highest scorer in the 1980s. The Slovak star had a prolific career, making an immediate impact in his rookie season in 1981, tallying 109 points. Šťastný continued to shine, recording six consecutive seasons with over 100 points from 1981 to 1986 and contributing 93 assists in the 1982 season, a franchise record that still stands.

Joe Sakic was the star when the franchise moved to Denver and reached its greatest heights, captaining the Stanley Cup champions of 1996 and 2001. Sakic was a pro-lific scorer, recording six seasons with over 100 points, and winning the Hart Memorial Trophy as league MVP in 2001, a season where he tallied 118 points and a league-high 12 game-winning goals. In addition to his consistency, Sakic was also as clutch as any player that ever lived: His eight overtime goals in the playoffs remain the most in NHL history.

Swedish superstar Peter Forsberg was best known for his exceptional playmaking and two-way skills, creating an immediate impact in the NHL and winning Rookie of the Year in 1995. Over his career, he achieved well over a point-per-game average, with 755 points in 591 regular-season games for the Nordiques/Avalanche, and was a vital piece of the Avalanche's first two Stanley Cup victories, totaling 35 points in 33 games across those two postseasons.

Patrick Roy is among the greatest goalies in NHL history, and while he might best be remembered for his time in Montreal, it was his stint in Colorado that solidified his place among the game's legends. Roy holds multiple records, including the most playoff wins by a goaltender with 151, 81 of which came in Denver. He won four Stanley Cup championships, two with the Canadiens and two with the Avalanche. In 2001, he captured his third Conn Smythe Trophy, highlighted by four shutouts across that postseason run.

#37
DETROIT PISTONS

×══ **Bob Lanier** ══×
×══ **Isiah Thomas** ══×
×══ **Joe Dumars** ══×
×══ **Chauncey Billups** ══×

In 1937, businessman Fred Zollner, whose Zollner Corporation manufactured pistons for car engines in Fort Wayne, Indiana, decided to sponsor a semipro basketball team at the request of his workers. That team turned professional in the 1940s, first joining the National Basketball League and then jumping to the Basketball Association of America. In 1949, Zollner brokered the merger of those two leagues to form the NBA from his kitchen table; suffice it to say, Fred Zollner is a name not enough sports fans remember, or even know.

The franchise would move to Detroit in 1957 but found almost no success in the NBA for decades, failing to win so much as a division title between 1957 and 1987, despite the presence of a handful of great players, including Hall of Famers Dave Bing and Bob Lanier. When those fortunes improved, however, they did so dramatically: Led by superstar Isiah Thomas and head coach Chuck Daly, the "Bad Boys" Pistons manufactured a run of sustained success, reaching three straight NBA Finals at the end of the eighties, winning twice, and cementing themselves among the most memorable teams in NBA history with their relentless, bruising style of play. A decade later, another era of winning play would emerge, led by Hall of Famer Chauncey Billups, in which the Pistons would advance to the Eastern Conference Finals in six consecutive seasons and shock a heavily favored Lakers team (featuring Shaquille O'Neal, Kobe Bryant, Karl Malone, and Gary Payton) to capture the franchise's third championship in 2004.

Bob Lanier was the first face of Detroit basketball, a big man who deserves to be better remembered than he is. In his finest season with the Pistons, 1973–74, Lanier finished third in MVP voting behind Kareem Abdul-Jabbar and Bob McAdoo. He was a seven-time all-star during his tenure in Detroit, with career averages of 22.7 points and 11.8 rebounds.

Isiah Thomas, meanwhile, is the greatest and most significant player in the history of the franchise. It has long been my contention that Thomas was the best of all the "little men" who dominated the game, including Allen Iverson and Steve Nash. (If one places Steph Curry in that category, clearly that would bump Zeke to the second spot.) Thomas's combination of leadership, tenacity, and toughness made him—inch for inch, and pound for pound—about as good as any player who ever lived. Thomas was a twelve-time all-star and a five-time

All-NBA selection, and had four seasons in which he averaged more than twenty points and ten assists.

Zeke's backcourt mate Joe Dumars belongs beside him, both literally and figuratively. The MVP of the 1989 NBA Finals, Dumars was among the top defensive guards of his generation, earning four first team All-Defense selections between 1989 and 1993. He also averaged over sixteen points for his career, and shot over 38 percent from three-point range, long before that skill was valued highly enough by the league. The Pistons would not have won without Isiah Thomas, and Thomas wouldn't have been able to do it without Dumars.

Known as Mr. Big Shot, Chauncey Billups earns the final spot here largely by leading the way to one of the more unexpected championships in the annals of the NBA. The MVP of those 2004 Finals against the Lakers, Billups was a five-time all-star and had his jersey number 1 retired by the Pistons in 2016.

#38
BALTIMORE RAVENS

× Jonathan Ogden ×
× Ray Lewis ×
× Ed Reed ×
× Lamar Jackson ×

While the unique circumstances of their beginnings cloud their being perceived as such, the Baltimore Ravens are actually the second-youngest franchise in the NFL. Despite bringing staff and personnel from Cleveland in 1996, the Ravens were technically considered an expansion team. (Thus, the history of the Cleveland Browns remained intact until their return to play in 1999—unlike the Colts, who took their history with them when they deserted their city and fans in the dead of night in 1984.) Thus, the Ravens have been around for just three decades, and through the entirety of that time have been among the most successful teams in the NFL. Dating to their first year of existence, the Ravens have the fifth-best overall record in the league, behind only the Patriots, Packers, Steelers, and Colts. In the first quarter of the twenty-first century, Baltimore made the playoffs sixteen times, winning seven division titles, seventeen playoff games, and two championships in as many Super Bowl appearances.

The foremost face of the franchise belongs to Ray

Lewis, the legendary linebacker known as much for his inspirational leadership as his fiery, dominating play on the field. Lewis was a twelve-time Pro Bowler and two-time Super Bowl champion, earning MVP honors in Super Bowl XXXV. That championship capped a season in which Lewis led one of the most dominant defenses the game has ever seen: The 2000 Ravens held opposing teams to 165 total points, beating the 1986 Bears record of 187 points for a sixteen-game season. As for Lewis, he would go on to record over 2,000 career tackles in Baltimore and was a two-time NFL Defensive Player of the Year.

For most of Lewis's tenure in Baltimore, he was teamed with the ball-hawking-est safety in football history. Ed Reed recorded 64 career interceptions, the most of any player to debut since 2000, earning nine Pro Bowl nods and five first-team All-Pro selections. Reed led the league in interceptions three times and was the NFL Defensive Player of the Year in 2004.

The staple on the other side of the football for those Ravens teams was Jonathan Ogden, the fourth overall pick in the 1996 draft, and thus the first draft pick in the history of the franchise. Standing six-nine and 345 pounds, the offensive tackle was the model of consistency and durability, and a nine-time All-Pro. When he was inducted into the Hall of Fame in 2013, he became the first player so honored who had played his entire career with the Ravens.

The fourth face belongs to Lamar Jackson, based as much on his potential future as on his past achievements. While still in the nascence of his career, the numbers the Heisman winner has put on the board so quickly have been historic and mind-boggling. At twenty-one, the youngest quarterback ever to start a playoff game, Jackson's 2019 campaign was one for the ages: He led the NFL in touchdown passes and set the all-time single season record for rushing yards by a quarterback. He was a unanimous choice for league MVP that season, the first of his two MVPs in his first five full seasons as a starter.

#39
MILWAUKEE BUCKS

✗ **Kareem Abdul-Jabbar** ✗
✗ **Jon McGlocklin** ✗
✗ **Sidney Moncrief** ✗
✗ **Giannis Antetokounmpo** ✗

In 1968, the NBA awarded a franchise to Milwaukee Professional Sports and Services, thus bringing the league back to the city thirteen years after their original team, the Hawks, departed for St. Louis (and ultimately Atlanta). The bad news for the Bucks was that, like most expansion franchises, they struggled mightily in their first season. The good news was, they picked the right season in which to struggle mightily. The prize for the first pick in the 1969 draft was Lew Alcindor out of UCLA, perhaps the greatest college prospect ever to enter the league. The Bucks drafted Alcindor and immediately saw their fortunes change: In his rookie season, the Bucks won 56 games, 29 more than the previous year. In the following offseason, Milwaukee would acquire an aging Oscar Robertson, who teamed with Alcindor to form one of the best teams the league had ever seen, winning 66 regular-season games and ultimately sweeping the Baltimore Bullets in the NBA Finals in only the Bucks' third season. Alcindor—who would change his name to Kareem

Abdul-Jabbar in 1971—would decide after six seasons that he wished to play in a larger market, leading to his tenure with Los Angeles. The Bucks would predictably wither as a result: Despite a handful of great players, coaches, and seasons, the franchise would not return to the Finals until 2021. Led by the Greek Freak, Giannis Antetokounmpo, Milwaukee would win its second championship half a century after its first, with Giannis scoring 50 points in the decisive Game 6 against the Phoenix Suns.

Abdul-Jabbar and Giannis are clear choices for this list, easily the two greatest players in franchise history. During his six seasons in Milwaukee, Abdul-Jabbar would average more than 30 points and 15 rebounds, winning three league MVP Awards, a Finals MVP, and Rookie of the Year in 1970. Giannis is, of course, still in the prime of his career, but has already stacked up Hall of Fame credentials, including two league MVPs, a Finals MVP, six first team All-NBA honors, and the Defensive Player of the Year award in 2020. The Greek Freak is one of three players, joining Michael Jordan and Hakeem Olajuwon, to ever win MVP and DPOY in the same season.

In the time after Abdul-Jabbar's departure, Milwaukee's top star was Sidney Moncrief, whose Hall of Fame career was marked by his two-way play and leadership. Moncrief played ten of his eleven NBA seasons for the Bucks, making five all-star teams and twice being named the league's Defensive Player of the Year.

Jon McGlocklin began his playing career with stops in Cincinnati and San Diego before being selected by the Bucks in the 1968 expansion draft. He spent eight seasons in Milwaukee, playing a key role on the championship team, averaging 15 points and 35 minutes during that postseason. He retired in 1976 as the last member of the Bucks' inaugural roster still on the team; his jersey number 14 was eventually retired by the franchise. But it is not his play that earns him this coveted slot. McGlocklin joined the Bucks broadcast team immediately upon completing his playing career and—now more than four decades later—has never stopped. Having played vital roles with the franchise for its entire existence, the much-loved McGlocklin is known by Milwaukee fans as Mr. Buck.

- ✖ **Marv Albert** ✖
- ✖ **Willis Reed** ✖
- ✖ **Walt Frazier** ✖
- ✖ **Patrick Ewing** ✖

The Knicks were among the founding franchises of the Basketball Association of America, the predecessor of the NBA, and actually played in the very first game in that league's history. In other words, the Knicks have been playing basketball every bit as long as there has been pro basketball in this country. Considering such, it is remarkable—and to their enormous and passionate fan base, highly frustrating—how little high-level success the franchise has had. Not only do they have just two titles to show for their nearly eighty years of existence (and none in the past half century), but in their entire history, the Knicks have had only one player win league MVP, and only five earn first team All-NBA honors. At the risk of belaboring the point, consider that the Rockets, Suns, and Spurs have all had multiple players win MVPs, despite joining the league decades later than New York. There is an enduring snakebitten element to the Knicks franchise, despite the receipt of more attention, coverage, and fandom than any NBA team aside from the Celtics and

Lakers. (If I sound bitter, perhaps it is because I am.) All of that said, the Knicks have a history as colorful as that of any team, filled with beloved players and coaches, and dotted with a multitude of unforgettable moments.

The first face of the franchise belongs to its only MVP, Willis Reed. He took the award in 1970 and was MVP of both Finals the franchise has won. Reed was the captain and unquestioned leader of the team through its most glorious era, advancing to three Finals in four years from 1970 to 1973, and stringing together six consecutive seasons with at least 48 wins. Reed's most famous moment came in Game 7 of the 1970 Finals, when he limped through the tunnel on a torn thigh muscle and into history in front of a raucous Madison Square Garden crowd on the night the franchise would win its first-ever championship. "Here comes Willis" is among the most famous collection of words in New York sports history.

The man who spoke those words deserves his space here as well. Marv Albert was the voice of the Knicks from 1967 through 2004, his calls synonymous with all the highs and lows of those generations. Albert, of course, also broadcast NBA games nationally on NBC, and later on TNT, and was known across the nation as "the voice of the NBA." Still, his connection to the fans in his hometown, as the announcer for both the Knicks and the NHL's Rangers, was as deep as any broadcaster's in America.

Meanwhile, the true star of that Game 7 in 1970 was

neither Reed nor Albert. Walt Frazier, the stylish point guard, authored perhaps the best Game 7 in league history with 36 points and 19 assists. In all, Frazier would play ten of his thirteen NBA seasons for the Knicks, making seven all-star teams and being named first-team All-NBA four times. He was named to the 75th Anniversary all-time NBA team in 2021 and has been a beloved and loquacious broadcaster for the Knicks for multiple decades; it is reasonable to say that Walt "Clyde" Frazier has had a longer and stronger relationship with New York fans than any other basketball player ever.

The final face of the Knicks has had a far more complicated relationship with the city, despite being the best player in franchise history. Patrick Ewing arrived in New York as the number one pick in 1985—after the first-ever draft lottery—with expectations even taller than his seven-foot frame. The truth is, he lived up to those: Ewing is the Knicks' all-time leader in games and minutes played, points, rebounds, and blocked shots. He brought the team within a game of the title in 1994 and, otherwise, generally had the bad fortune of running into Michael Jordan too many times (five, to be exact). Ewing's introverted personality wasn't always a great fit with the largest media market in the league, and the relationship he forged with the fans never ran as deep as it did for other Knicks players. But Ewing was a first-ballot Hall of Famer and deserves to be remembered as the best player the franchise ever had.

#41
INDIANAPOLIS COLTS

× **Gino Marchetti** ×
× **Johnny Unitas** ×
× **Marvin Harrison** ×
× **Peyton Manning** ×

The history of the Colts is as rocky as it is rich, replete with stops and starts, soaring highs, and one lowdown desertion that ranks with the worst of its kind in sports. The Colts originally played in the AAFC, but upon joining the NFL in 1950, they struggled so badly—competitively and financially—that they disbanded after just one season. Three years later, local owner Carroll Rosenbloom won the rights to bring a new team to the NFL. Under the guidance of head coach Weeb Ewbank and quarterbacked by the legendary Johnny Unitas, the Baltimore Colts won NFL championships in 1958 and 1959, and then after Ewbank departed, won another in 1968. After the AFL-NFL merger, the team won their first Super Bowl title after the 1970 season.

The most hated words in Baltimore sports history are *Mayflower Transit,* the name of an Indianapolis-based moving company that brought the Colts to Indiana. Their vans arrived in Baltimore on the morning of March 29, 1984, loaded all the team's belongings, and by midday, departed for Indianapolis, leaving practically nothing of the Colts organization behind. The move, while infamous, has been largely successful on the field, with the team's golden era in the 2000s under quarterback Peyton Manning. From 2003 to 2009, the Colts had seven consecutive seasons with twelve or more victories, a first in NFL history. They won five straight AFC South titles from 2003 to 2007 and made nine consecutive playoff appearances, winning Super Bowl XLI.

Chronologically, the first face of the Colts belongs to Gino Marchetti, Hall of Fame defensive lineman, who played in Baltimore from 1953 to 1966. Marchetti's tenacity and skill earned him eleven Pro Bowl selections and seven first-team All-Pro nods as the central figure in a defense that ranked in the top five four times between 1958 and 1966.

Unitas and Manning are, of course, easy inclusions in this exercise; in fact, I would argue that no team in the NFL has ever had two quarterbacks as historically great as these two, considering there is no credible list of the ten greatest ever to play that does not include them both. Unitas was a ten-time Pro Bowler and three-time MVP who led the Colts to three championships. Known for his clutch performances and leadership, Unitas rewrote the NFL record books, and his precision passing and football IQ revolutionized the position. Manning, of course, had an impact on the franchise and the sport that was in every way comparable to his legendary predecessor. Playing in Indianapolis from 1998 to 2010, Manning won league MVP four times in seven seasons spanning 2003–09, leading the Colts to their most recent title in Super Bowl XLI.

Manning's favorite target rounds out this list. Marvin Harrison was an eight-time Pro Bowler and three-time first-team All-Pro who set numerous records, including the single-season receptions record (143) and four consecutive 100-catch seasons (1999–2002). Alongside Manning, Harrison formed one of the most potent quarterback-wide receiver duos in NFL history, finishing with 1,102 receptions for 14,580 yards and 128 touchdown catches, all for the Colts.

#42
CHICAGO CUBS

⚔ **Ernie Banks** ⚔
⚔ **Ron Santo** ⚔
⚔ **Harry Caray** ⚔
⚔ **Ryne Sandberg** ⚔

In the history of American team sports, there have been few championship celebrations more anticipated or wholeheartedly enjoyed than that of the Chicago Cubs winning the 2016 World Series. It was a title that was literally multiple lifetimes in the making.

The Cubs were a founding member of the National League in 1876, first known as the White Stockings, and eventually renamed the Cubs in 1904. In the early years of the twentieth century, they were a powerhouse, winning 116 games in 1906 (which remains the most all-time in the regular season, tied with the 2001 Mariners) and then back-to-back championships in 1907 and 1908, becoming the first major league team to win the World Series twice. It was around then that the good times ceased: It would be 108 years before the Cubs would once again hoist the trophy. In fact, the team would not even appear in a World Series from 1945 to 2015. In that magical 2016 run, the Cubs would overcome a three-games-to-one deficit to defeat the Cleveland Indians, the first team to overcome such a deficit in the World Series in over three decades. On November 4, the city of Chicago held a victory parade and rally for the Cubs that began at Wrigley Field, headed down Lake Shore Drive, and ended in Grant Park. The city estimated that over five million people attended the parade and rally, which made it one of the largest recorded gatherings in the history of planet Earth.

Because of the short-lived tenure of the group of players who won that title, no member of the championship team deserves a space representing this historic franchise. The best player on the team was Kris Bryant—the NL MVP that season—who appeared on the verge of superstardom; that destiny was not fulfilled, and he played only seven seasons for the Cubs. Despite the lack of high-level winning, though, the franchise boasts more worthy representatives.

It begins with Mr. Cub, Ernie Banks, a legendary shortstop and first baseman who won back-to-back NL MVPs in 1958–59. He hit 512 home runs, including five seasons at shortstop in which he hit 40 or more homers. Banks's infectious attitude and love for the game ("Let's play two!") earned him the reputation as one of baseball's great ambassadors. He holds multiple Cubs career records, including games (2,528) and total bases (4,706), and was inducted into the Hall of Fame in 1977.

Ryne Sandberg is next. The Hall of Fame second baseman was a ten-time all-star, nine-time Gold Glove winner, seven-time Silver Slugger recipient, and NL MVP in 1984, the season he led the Cubs to their first postseason appearance since 1945. He had a career .285 batting average with 282 home runs and 1,061 RBI—and was the most beloved athlete in Chicago up until Michael Jordan came along and changed absolutely everything.

Ron Santo is deserving of his place here as well, both for his play and his passion for the franchise, which shone through as he became a beloved and iconic broadcaster after his playing days. Meanwhile, as a third baseman, Santo was a nine-time all-star and five-time Gold Glove winner who sported a keen eye, leading the NL in walks on four occasions. Despite being inducted into the Hall of Fame only posthumously, his impact on the Cubs franchise was undeniable.

The final face here is more a voice than anything else, and it belonged to Harry Caray. The broadcaster's remarkable career included a lengthy stay in St. Louis, followed by stops with the Athletics and White Sox, before finishing with sixteen unforgettable seasons behind the mic for the Cubs (1982–97). It is not hyperbole to say that Harry was the most beloved person in Chicago during those years, inclusive of Jordan, Mike Ditka, Mayor Daley, or anyone else. In fact, he was named the Mayor of Rush Street, and was perhaps the greatest marketing instrument any baseball team has ever had. His rendition of "Take Me Out to the Ball Game" during the seventh inning stretch was so iconic that the team carries on the tradition to this day. (As an aside, for all the extraordinary opportunities I have been presented during my career, nothing has ever topped the honor of singing that song in the booth that Harry made famous—and nothing ever will.)

#43
CHICAGO WHITE SOX

× Shoeless Joe Jackson ×

× Nellie Fox ×

× Ken "Hawk" Harrelson ×

× Frank Thomas ×

I t is impossible to tell the story of the Chicago White Sox, a charter member of the American League in 1901, without covering the lowest moment in the history of baseball. Thirteen years after the franchise won its first World Series in 1906—with a defensive-oriented team known as the Hitless Wonders—and two years after it won its second, various members of the 1919 White Sox conspired with gamblers to throw that season's World Series against the Reds. These architects of the most serious gambling scandal in American sports history, known to eternity as the Black Sox, tarnished the reputation of baseball. They went to trial and were ultimately acquitted—but were banned from professional baseball. The aftermath of the scandal resulted in significant reforms and the establishment of a new commissioner's office to restore integrity to the game.

The greatest player on those championship Sox teams, and among the great players of his era, was Shoeless Joe Jackson. The outfielder was implicated in the gambling scandal and banned for life from the game despite going to his grave denying any involvement. In our estimation, there is sufficient doubt about his role in that 1919 World Series that Shoeless Joe deserves his place here as one of the faces of the franchise. During his six seasons with Chicago, he totaled 829 hits in 648 games; he batted .340 for the White Sox, which remains the franchise career record.

Scrappy second baseman Nellie Fox is next on this list, an all-star in twelve of thirteen seasons from 1951 to 1963 and three-time Gold Glove winner known for his defensive prowess and clutch hitting. He won the AL MVP in 1959, leading the White Sox to the World Series. Fox's small stature belied his impact on the field, where he compiled more than 2,600 hits and played a superb second base, earning him induction into the Baseball Hall of Fame in 1997.

Frank Thomas weighed in about a hundred pounds heavier than Fox did. Built more like a tight end than a first baseman, Thomas was a brilliantly disciplined hitter who dominated the American League in the 1990s. Known for his power and keen eye, blasting 521 home runs while amassing over 100 walks in ten different seasons, the Big Hurt won back-to-back MVPs in 1993 and 1994.

The final representative of this franchise is Ken "Hawk" Harrelson, who broadcast their games from 1982 to 2018. Hawk was known for commentary that was equal parts passionate and insightful, and beloved for his colorful catchphrases, including "You can put it on the board . . . YES!" Harrelson's enthusiasm and loyalty shone through his years of broadcasting, particularly during stretches of seasons when White Sox fans had very little to celebrate. In 2020, Harrelson was named the recipient of the Ford C. Frick Award, presented annually to one broadcaster for "major contributions to baseball."

44

HOUSTON ROCKETS

× **Rudy Tomjanovich** ×
× **Moses Malone** ×
× **Hakeem Olajuwon** ×
× **James Harden** ×

The San Diego Rockets were formed as an expansion team in 1967 and relocated to Houston four years later—and while it would be nearly a decade before they completed a season with a winning record, the early era of Rockets basketball had a good deal of high-level post-season success. In their second year as a franchise, they selected Elvin Hayes with the first pick in the draft and made the playoffs, increasing their regular-season win total from 15 to 37.

Some eight years later, the Rockets would acquire Moses Malone, who would ultimately lead them on one of the more improbable playoff runs in NBA history. In the 1980–81 season, the Rockets finished 40–42, with Malone averaging 27.8 points and 14.8 rebounds. Despite the losing record, the Rockets would not be stopped in the Western Conference playoffs, advancing to the NBA Finals after a decisive Game 5 win over the Kings behind 36 points from Malone. Houston would lose the series in six games to Boston, but that Rockets team remains the last to reach the NBA Finals with a losing regular-season record.

Malone is an easy first choice for the franchise, having won two league MVP awards in Houston and establishing himself as one of the greatest centers of all time. The same distinction applies to Hakeem Olajuwon, obviously, who played seventeen of his eighteen NBA seasons for the Rockets, leading Houston to back-to-back championships in 1994 and 1995, being named Finals MVP in both years. The Dream was named to twelve All-NBA teams, winning league MVP in 1994. Olajuwon remains the league's all-time leader in blocked shots (3,830), and on March 29, 1990, he registered one of only four quadruple-doubles in NBA history with 18 points, 16 rebounds, 10 assists, and 11 blocks against Milwaukee.

Younger NBA fans may only recognize Rudy Tomjanovich as the coach of those Olajuwon-led championship teams, where he compiled 503 wins in his twelve seasons at the helm—the most coaching wins in franchise history. (Tomjanovich was so respected as a head coach that he was selected to lead USA Basketball and won the gold medal in the 2000 Olympics in Sydney.) However, before any of that, Rudy T was a fine player for the Rockets: The second overall pick in the 1970 draft out of Michigan, he played his entire eleven-year career for the franchise, making five all-star teams and having his jersey number 45 retired.

James Harden rounds out this quartet, having compiled seasons in Houston that compare favorably with
practically any in league history. During his eight full
seasons with the Rockets, Harden never averaged fewer
than 25 points, with three seasons over 30, including a
36.1 average in 2018–19; only Michael Jordan and Wilt
Chamberlain (five times) ever averaged more. Harden was
All-NBA in seven of his eight seasons in Houston and was
named league MVP in 2018.

#45
TAMPA BAY LIGHTNING

× **Vincent Lecavalier** ×
× **Martin St. Louis** ×
× **Steven Stamkos** ×
× **Nikita Kucherov** ×

When the NHL awarded an expansion franchise to the city of Tampa in 1992, the jokes wrote themselves: There is no month on the calendar in which the average temperature in Tampa is below 70 degrees, rendering the city a fascinating choice for a sport that is played on the ice. Soon enough, the weather ceased to be the primary concern: The Lightning reached the playoffs just once in their first ten seasons. The savior of the franchise proved to be Bill Davidson, a Detroit businessman best known as the owner of the Pistons. Finally, under the leadership of Davidson and coach John Tortorella, the Lightning got it right. Tampa finished their second season with a winning record and won its first division title in 2003, the eleventh season in franchise history. They would take their success to the greatest of heights the following year, raising the Stanley Cup for the first time of what is now three times.

Star center Vincent Lecavalier played a pivotal role in that first championship, tallying 16 points in 23 playoff games. Lecavalier had a long and legendary tenure in Tampa from 1998 to 2013, winning the Maurice "Rocket" Richard Trophy for most goals in a season in 2006–07. He recorded 383 goals and 491 assists for a total of 874 points in 1,037 games with the Lightning, and his loyalty to the franchise solidified his status as one of the most beloved players in Lightning history.

Martin St. Louis was the star of that first title team in 2004, winning the Hart Memorial Trophy for league MVP that season. Known for his speed, skill, and clutch performances, St. Louis had a stellar tenure from 2000 to 2014, winning the Art Ross Trophy as the league's top goal scorer twice—a remarkable nine years apart (2004 and 2013).

Tampa's more recent championship era has come in just the last few years, highlighted by back-to-back Stanley Cup championships in 2020 and 2021, with teams led by prolific center and captain Steven Stamkos, the first overall pick in the 2008 draft. Stamkos is a two-time league goals leader, who by the end of the 2023–24 season had recorded 555 career goals and 582 assists, good for 1,137 points in 1,082 games for the organization. In 2023, his second-to-last season in Tampa, Stamkos received the Mark Messier Award for exhibiting the best leadership in the NHL.

Dynamic right winger Nikita Kucherov rounds out the foursome for Tampa Bay, twice leading the NHL in points, being named league MVP after his first such season in 2019; he tallied an astronomical 100 assists in the 2023–24 season, as did the Oilers' Connor McDavid that same year, a number that had not been reached in the twenty-first century. During Tampa's back-to-back championship runs, Kucherov tallied 66 points in 48 postseason games.

#46
WASHINGTON COMMANDERS

✕ Sammy Baugh ✕
✕ Jack Kent Cooke ✕
✕ Joe Gibbs ✕
✕ Darrell Green ✕

Long before there was the Boston—or New England—Patriots, pro football was played in Boston by a team founded as the Boston Braves in 1932. The team would change its nickname to the Redskins the following year and move to Washington in 1937 as one of the foundational franchises of the sport. As of the conclusion of the 2023 NFL season, only four franchises have more wins in the history of the NFL: the Packers, Bears, Giants, and Steelers. The heyday of the franchise consists of two glorious decades, separated by nearly half a century. From 1936 through 1945, Washington played in the NFL championship game six times, winning twice. Those teams were led, primarily, by Hall of Fame head coach Ray Flaherty—who is credited with inventing the screen pass—and Sammy Baugh, the greatest quarterback of the game's early era. The second golden decade in Washington lasted from 1982 through 1991 and was led by flamboyant owner Jack Kent Cooke (who also owned the Los Angeles Lakers and oversaw six trips to the NBA Finals) and Hall of

Fame coach Joe Gibbs. Otherwise, the franchise's history has been mostly messy, including decades of controversy over the team's nickname, which finally changed in 2020, and a variety of scandals and general fan disgust regarding longtime owner Daniel Snyder, who sold the team in 2023.

"Slinging" Sammy Baugh is the obvious first face of this franchise, a genuine legend from the foundational years of football who played all sixteen of his NFL seasons in Washington. Baugh absolutely begins the thread of the game's legendary quarterbacks, which extends through Otto Graham, Johnny Unitas, Bart Starr, and others before arriving at the iconic names of the Super Bowl era. Baugh was not only the best quarterback of his day but was also a dominant safety and the league's best punter; in 1943, he led the NFL in pass completions, interceptions as a defender, and in punts (50), punt yardage (2,295), and yards per punt (45.9). In 1963, he was among seventeen players inducted into the inaugural Pro Football Hall of Fame class.

Jack Kent Cooke comes next, one of the most influential and visible sports owners of his time. In fact, he was well ahead of his time; long before Jerry Jones or Robert Kraft, the most prestigious suite to be spotted in was Cooke's. Michael Wilbon, who has covered sports in our nation's capital as long and well as practically any journalist, once said, "He was the best owner in the history of sports. Not pro football, of all sports."

During the dozen years of Joe Gibbs's first tenure with Washington, he went 124–60, winning three Super Bowls, advancing to a fourth, and compiling an astonishing 16–5 record in the postseason. He remains the only coach to win three Super Bowls with three different quarterbacks. Gibbs was voted into the Pro Football Hall of Fame in 1996, then returned to coach the team again for four more seasons. In his second tenure, Washington reached the playoffs twice—once more than they had in the eleven seasons after his first retirement.

Darrell Green played in Washington from 1983 to 2002, with speed and durability that were the stuff of legend, earning him seven Pro Bowl selections and four All-Pro nods. In his twenty seasons (a record for defensive backs) he recorded 54 career interceptions, returning six for touchdowns, and was inducted into the Pro Football Hall of Fame in 2008.

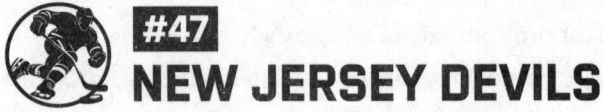

#47
NEW JERSEY DEVILS

✖ **Lou Lamoriello** ✖
✖ **Martin Brodeur** ✖
✖ **Scott Stevens** ✖
✖ **Patrik Eliáš** ✖

The New Jersey Devils, founded in Kansas City as the Scouts and then shipped to Denver as the Colorado Rockies before settling in the Garden State in 1982, can neatly divide their history into two periods: before and after Lou Lamoriello. Consider: Over two seasons in Kansas City, the franchise finished 27–110–23; in six seasons in Denver, they never won more than 22 games; in 1983, Wayne Gretzky suggested the newly minted New Jersey Devils were a "Mickey Mouse organization." Simply put, they stunk, and they always had, until they hired Lamoriello as team president in 1987.

Almost instantly, the fortunes of the franchise changed: The Devils made the playoffs all but three times between 1988 and 2012—including a stretch of thirteen seasons in a row—and finished with a winning record every season from 1992 to 2010. They would make five trips to the Stanley Cup Final under Lamoriello's leadership, winning three championships. Lamoriello was a true giant of the sport, who would also serve as general manager for Team

USA in the World Cup of Hockey in 1996, in which the US won the championship, as well as for the 1998 Winter Olympics. He also played a key role in negotiating the settlement of the NHL lockout in 2005. In 2009 Lamoriello was inducted into the Hall of Fame in the Builders category, which includes coaches, general managers, commentators, team owners, and others who have helped build the game. Few executives have been more dramatically impactful in recent NHL history.

Among the most important moves Lamoriello would make came in the first round of the 1990 draft with the selection of goaltender Martin Brodeur, who became a four-time Vezina Trophy winner. Brodeur holds numerous NHL records, including most career wins (691) and shutouts (125), the vast majority of which came in his twenty-one-year Devils career. Brodeur also won three Stanley Cup championships with the Devils. Known for puck-handling skills so accomplished the league changed its rules to reduce their potency, his durability and unorthodox style contributed to Brodeur being routinely listed among the five greatest goaltenders in the history of the game.

Acquired via transfer compensation from St. Louis, defenseman Scott Stevens was the perfect fit for the defense-minded Devils of the 1990s. Stevens captained New Jersey to three Stanley Cup championships and was awarded the Conn Smythe Trophy in 2000. Known for his physical play and leadership, Stevens recorded 430 points in 956 games with the Devils and is revered for his defensive prowess. His impact extended beyond statistics, embodying grit and toughness on the ice. By the time he retired, he had played the most games of any defenseman in history.

Patrik Eliáš arrived shortly after the two anchors of the New Jersey defense to provide exactly the scoring punch the franchise needed. The left winger skated twenty seasons for the Devils and remains the team's all-time leading scorer with 408 goals and 617 assists for a total of 1,025 points in 1,240 games. He won two Stanley Cup championships with the Devils and had his number 26 retired by the franchise in 2018.

48

OKLAHOMA CITY THUNDER

✖ **Jack Sikma** ✖
✖ **Gary Payton** ✖
✖ **Kevin Durant** ✖
✖ **Russell Westbrook** ✖

For the first forty-one years of its existence, the NBA franchise now based in Oklahoma City represented Seattle, cultivating one of the most passionate fan bases the sport has ever had. The team, then known as the SuperSonics, joined the league as an expansion club in 1967. In its early history, the Sonics were led by such legends as player/coach Lenny Wilkens and Hall of Famer Bill Russell, who coached the Sonics for four seasons in the mid-1970s. It wasn't until late in that decade, however, that the franchise truly hit its stride. With Wilkens back as head coach, the Sonics made the NBA Finals in back-to-back years, winning it all in 1979. A generation later, in 1996, Seattle would once again win the Western Conference, only to run into the 72-win Chicago Bulls, who took the Finals in six games.

Among the franchise's final actions before they relocated to OKC (after a lengthy and nasty legal battle) was the selection of Kevin Durant number two overall in the 2007 draft, and then Russell Westbrook at number four the following year. With their young core, the newly renamed Thunder quickly became a powerhouse, qualifying for the playoffs during the 2009–10 season, winning their first division title the following year, and then making a Finals run in the 2011–12 season. This marked the fourth trip to the NBA Finals in franchise history, and first in OKC. The championship round ended in a Game 5 loss to Miami as LeBron James claimed his first NBA title.

Jack Sikma was the star of the only NBA Finals the franchise ever won while in Seattle. The versatile center known for his shooting touch and rebounding was a player ahead of his time, spreading the floor with his outside shooting while standing 6-foot-11. Sikma was a seven-time all-star and received MVP votes in five seasons. In the 1979 Finals against the Washington Bullets, Sikma averaged 15.8 points and 14.8 rebounds; the year before, Sikma had 21 points and 11 rebounds in a hard-fought Game 7 defeat against the same Bullets team. An ironman of sorts—he competed in 784 of the 807 games (including playoffs) that Seattle played across his nine seasons with the team. In 2019, Sikma finally received his deserved place in the Hall of Fame.

The Seattle teams of the 1990s featured Gary Payton, known as the Glove, among the greatest defensive guards in the history of the sport. Payton was a nine-time all-star and was the first point guard ever to win Defensive Player of the Year in 1996, the season in which he led the Sonics to the Finals. For seven consecutive years he finished in the top 6 of Defensive Player of the Year voting. Over his thirteen seasons with the Sonics, Payton averaged 18.2 points and 7.5 assists, while his legendary trash talk earned him the fourth-most technical fouls in the record books.

Durant is, of course, easily the greatest player in franchise history, though his personal history with the organization is a complicated one. His play on the court was beyond rebuke: Durant led the league in scoring four of five seasons between 2010 and 2014. He also won the MVP award in 2014, averaging 32.0 points, ingratiating himself to practically everyone with his acceptance speech in which he described his mother as "the real MVP." Durant was hugely instrumental in leading the Thunder to the NBA Finals in 2012 and was well on his way to becoming a similar sort of franchise icon as Kobe Bryant for the Lakers or Dirk Nowitzki for the Mavs. You no doubt know what happened next: After losing to the Warriors in the Conference Finals in 2016, he departed OKC and joined up with Golden State, forming a super team that dominated the league for three years. It was a decision that has been as hotly debated as practically any in recent sports memory; thus the complicated nature of his legacy in OKC. What is not in question, however, is that Durant was the best player the franchise ever had and most certainly belongs on this list.

So does his longtime running mate, Russell Westbrook,

who was an eight-time all-star in OKC and earned the MVP award in 2017 after averaging 31.6 points, 10.7 rebounds, and 10.4 assists, becoming the first since Oscar Robertson in 1961–62 to average a triple-double for an entire season. He won two scoring titles (2015 and 2017) and two assists titles (2018 and 2019). Westbrook played eleven seasons for the Thunder after their move to Oklahoma City, more than any player to date.

#49
MINNESOTA TWINS

× **Walter Johnson** ×
× **Harmon Killebrew** ×
× **Rod Carew** ×
× **Kirby Puckett** ×

T he franchise long known as the Twins was first known—and theatrically immortalized in the musical *Damn Yankees*—as the Washington Nationals or Senators, founded in 1901 as one of the eight original teams in the American League. The Senators regularly finished near the bottom of the league standings; so well known were their struggles that the musical depicted them taking drastic measures to overcome the sluggers from New York.

The franchise moved to Minnesota's Twin Cities, from which they derived their new name, in 1961 and immediately endured decades of mediocrity—and worse. From their relocation until they finally broke through as World Series champions in 1987, the Twins would win just one pennant and two Western Division crowns. The golden era of Minnesota baseball came in the late 1980s and early 1990s, with teams led by Hall of Famer Kirby Puckett. The Twins captured two championships and won ninety or more games three times in the six seasons spanning

1987–92. In 1984, the Twins were sold by Calvin Griffith to billionaire banker Carl Pohlad, who promised to keep the franchise in Minnesota, and thus was granted the team despite a larger offer from a New York real estate magnate by the name of Donald Trump.

The first face of this franchise, chronologically or otherwise, belongs to Walter Johnson. Known as the Big Train. Feared for his blazing fastball, he was a twelve-time 20-game winner who recorded 417 wins, 3,509 strikeouts, and a career 2.17 ERA. Johnson won three Triple Crowns and threw 110 shutouts, an MLB record that still stands and always will.

Harmon Killebrew was the first Minnesota baseball icon, owner of six home run titles and AL MVP in 1969. Known for his prodigious power, he hit between 40 and 49 home runs in eight seasons, finishing with 573, fifth all-time at the date of his retirement. His powerful swing and offensive prowess earned him the nickname Killer, while his leadership and sportsmanship made him a beloved figure; he was inducted into the Hall of Fame in 1984.

Among the most beloved (and imitated) players of his generation, Rod Carew played his first twelve seasons in Minnesota. With his distinctive batting stance, Carew was a surgical hitter; he was a seven-time AL batting champion (all in Minnesota), batting .334 in his Twins career (the highest in franchise history). He won the AL Rookie of the Year award in 1967 and captured the AL MVP in 1977 before departing for the Angels two years later; in 1987, the Twins would retire his jersey number 29.

Last, but certainly not least, is Puckett, a ten-time all-star and six-time Gold Glove winner during his tenure from 1984 through 1995, when his career was cut short by a condition that cost him his vision in one eye. Puckett was the unquestioned leader and star on the championship teams in 1987 and 1991, totaling 30 hits across 24 postseason games while making one of the most legendary catches in World Series history during Game 6 of the 1991 Fall Classic. Known for his exceptional defense, efficient hitting, and infectious enthusiasm for the game, Puckett compiled over 2,300 hits and was inducted into the Hall of Fame on the first ballot in 2001.

PHILADELPHIA EAGLES

× **Chuck Bednarik** ×
× **Reggie White** ×
× **Brian Dawkins** ×
× **Jason Kelce** ×

In the early 1930s, a Philadelphia businessman named Bert Bell forever changed American sports as we know them. After being granted an expansion franchise by the NFL, Bell founded the Philadelphia Eagles in 1933, joining the league the same year as their in-state rival, the Pittsburgh Steelers. The Eagles lost their first game 56–0 against the New York Giants and did not significantly better their fortunes for quite some time, never winning more than five games in any of their first eleven seasons. Perhaps motivated by these struggles, Bell proposed an annual college draft to equalize talent across the league—a then-revolutionary concept in professional sports in which teams select players in inverse order of the prior season's standings. The goal was to increase fan interest by guaranteeing that even the worst teams could annually infuse top talent, a practice that is, of course, now widely utilized throughout practically all American team sports. Bell was, in fact, a hugely significant figure in the early years of football, having quarterbacked the University of

Pennsylvania to the Rose Bowl as a collegian; he would ultimately become the NFL's second commissioner, serving from 1946 until his death in 1959.

Known as Concrete Charlie, Chuck Bednarik was the first superstar in Eagles history, a versatile and fierce player who excelled at both linebacker and center. During his career from 1949 to 1962, he was an eight-time Pro Bowler and two-time NFL champion who epitomized toughness with his iron man mentality, highlighted by twenty career interceptions on defense and as a key blocker on offense. Bednarik's presence and leadership made him a revered figure in Eagles history as the last of the NFL's sixty-minute men.

During his tenure with Philadelphia from 1985 to 1992, Reggie White may well have been the most dominant defensive end the game has ever seen. The Minister of Defense amassed 124 sacks in 120 games with the Eagles, including a franchise-record 21 in the 1987 season. White was named a first-team All-Pro in six consecutive seasons with the Eagles (1986–91), three of which resulted in playoff trips on the back of Buddy Ryan's legendary defense.

Known as Weapon X for complicated reasons that relate to the popular Marvel character Wolverine, safety Brian Dawkins played in Philadelphia from 1996 to 2008, earning nine Pro Bowl nods and four first-team All-Pro selections. In Philadelphia, Dawkins recorded 34 interceptions, 32 forced fumbles, and 21 sacks, but his impact transcended statistics. His tenacity, leadership, and ferocious style made him a fan favorite and earned him a place in the Pro Football Hall of Fame in 2018.

Jason Kelce is the rarest of sports rarities: a center who became the most beloved member of his NFL team. Kelce's dynamic personality and leadership made him an icon, particularly after the Eagles' shocking championship run in 2018, culminating with a victory over the Patriots in Super Bowl LII. Kelce earned six first-team All-Pro selections across his last seven seasons, and his proficiency in the Tush Push, his team's unique take on the quarterback sneak, created one of the most unstoppable plays in football history.

#51
PHILADELPHIA FLYERS

⚔ **Bernie Parent** ⚔
⚔ **Bobby Clarke** ⚔
⚔ **Eric Lindros** ⚔
⚔ **Claude Giroux** ⚔

They say that the more things change, the more they stay the same. And when it comes to hockey in Philadelphia, the sentiment most certainly applies. Since 1967, the team known as the Broad Street Bullies has played on Broad Street in two different arenas. Their colors and logo have never changed, the orange and white influenced by the University of Texas, the alma mater of one of the club's founders. And the image of the club has, generally, reflected the hardscrabble persona of the city it represents, never more so than when they earned their legendary nickname, and when they won their only championships.

In January of 1973, the *Philadelphia Bulletin* began referring to the team as the Broad Street Bullies, an intimidating bunch that did plenty of brawling, along with a good deal of winning. It was the following season in which the Flyers won their first-ever Stanley Cup, the first of two they would raise in consecutive years. In that 1974 postseason, the Flyers became the first expansion team to eliminate an Original Six team when it dispatched the Rangers in the semifinals, and then did it again by taking down Bobby Orr's Bruins to win the championship.

The backbone of those title teams was goaltender Bernie Parent, who *was* with the franchise from its beginning in 1967. Parent was a two-time Vezina Trophy winner and two-time Conn Smythe Trophy recipient. Known for his dynamic style in the net and calm demeanor under pressure, Parent was a cornerstone of the Flyers' success throughout the 1970s.

Legendary center Bobby Clarke provided much of Philadelphia's scoring punch after arriving in 1969. Clarke was a three-time Hart Memorial Trophy winner as league MVP and captained the two-time Stanley Cup champions. Known for his strong leadership on and off the ice, he recorded over 1,200 points while embodying the gritty style that became the team's hallmark. Clarke's impact extended well beyond statistics and into shaping the Flyers' identity. He left a legacy in Philadelphia and the hockey world and was inducted into the Hall of Fame in 1987.

The acquisition of dominant center Eric Lindros was of great consequence across the NHL; drafted number one overall by the Quebec Nordiques in 1991, Lindros refused to play for them, ultimately being traded to Philadelphia and making his debut in 1992. While his tenure with the Flyers, and in the NHL, was cut short by repeated concussions, Lindros was unstoppable when available, winning MVP in the 1994–95 season with a league-high 70 points in 46 games. During his eight injury-plagued seasons in Philadelphia, he tallied 659 points in 486 games.

Claude Giroux claims the final piece to this puzzle after playing the first fifteen seasons of his career in Philadelphia, becoming the longest-tenured captain (ten seasons) in team history. Giroux led the Flyers to the play-offs on eight occasions and totaled the second-most points (900) and assists (609) in franchise history, behind only Bobby Clarke in each category.

#52
DENVER NUGGETS

⚒ **Dan Issel** ⚒
⚒ **Alex English** ⚒
⚒ **Carmelo Anthony** ⚒
⚒ **Nikola Jokić** ⚒

The year 1967 was monumental for sports in this nation, beginning in January with what is now known as Super Bowl I, then the National Hockey League literally doubling in size that fall. Around that same time, with significantly less fanfare, a new league was born: the American Basketball Association. An upstart alternative to the NBA, the ABA featured a variety of quirky, innovative rules, and a red-white-and-blue ball that became synonymous with the league. There were eleven teams in the original ABA, among them the Denver Rockets, a team that had planned to play in Kansas City, but moved to Denver before playing a single game due to the other city's lack of an arena. Initially, the Rockets were called the Larks but also changed that before ever taking the court. In 1974, the name was changed to the Nuggets for the ABA's final two seasons (they would lose to Julius Erving and the Nets in the last ABA Finals). The Nuggets were one of four ABA teams to merge with the NBA in 1976. In the NBA, the Nuggets have had multiple eras of sustained success: They made the playoffs in nine straight seasons from 1982 to 1990 and then in ten straight seasons from 2004 to 2013. In 1994, center Dikembe Mutombo recorded 31 blocks in a five-game series with the Sonics, making the Nuggets the first eight seed to upset a one seed in NBA playoff history. But it was not until 2023, led by Serbian superstar Nikola Jokić, that the Nuggets finally broke through, becoming the last of the four surviving ABA teams to reach the NBA Finals, and only the second to win it (after the Spurs).

Dan Issel was the first star of Denver basketball, beginning his Nuggets career in 1975. He was a key figure in the Nuggets' early success, averaging 20.7 points and 8.3 rebounds; he remains the second-leading scorer in franchise history (16,589 points). After his playing career, Issel would return to Denver as head coach, leading the Nuggets to what was the biggest upset in NBA playoff history in 1994 when they became the first eighth seed to bounce a number one seed (the Seattle SuperSonics) from the playoffs.

Known for his smooth scoring ability and versatility as a forward, Alex English was a key figure in the Nuggets' high-octane offenses of the 1980s. He led the league in scoring during the 1982–83 season with an average of 28.4 points and was an all-star in eight consecutive seasons from 1982–89. English remains the franchise's all-time leading scorer, finishing his Nuggets career with 21,645 points.

Selected third overall in the 2003 NBA Draft from Syracuse, Carmelo Anthony quickly established himself as a prolific scorer in the NBA. He averaged over 20 points in every season in Denver, peaking during 2006–07 with 28.9. Melo led the Nuggets to seven straight playoff appearances and the Western Conference Finals in 2009.

Chronologically, the franchise has saved its best for last: Nikola Jokić is easily the greatest player in franchise history and appears destined to finish his career ranked among the immortals of the sport. A second-round pick in 2014, Jokić has made six All-NBA teams and won three MVP awards. Most meaningfully, in 2023, Joker led the Nuggets to their first-ever championship and was named Finals MVP after averaging 30 points and 14 rebounds in the five-game victory over the Heat, becoming the first-ever player to lead an entire postseason in total points, total rebounds, and total assists.

#53

LOS ANGELES RAMS

✖ **Deacon Jones** ✖
✖ **Merlin Olsen** ✖
✖ **Kurt Warner** ✖
✖ **Aaron Donald** ✖

Most readers, no doubt, are well aware that the Rams have won NFL championships in two cities: in St. Louis, with a dramatic last-second tackle that preserved a win over the Titans in Super Bowl XXXIV, and then in Los Angeles in Super Bowl LVI, which was capped off by another legendary defensive stop by Aaron Donald. However, it is likely that only the most knowledgeable are aware that the franchise won its first title as the Cleveland Rams in 1945, a year before moving to LA. Thus, the Rams are the only franchise in pro football to win championships representing three different cities.

The golden era of Rams football was the early 1950s, when they were the only professional sports team in Southern California and Bob Waterfield and Norm Van Brocklin led the Rams to four NFL championship games and one title (1951), between 1949 and 1955. Their wide-open offense, featuring Hall of Fame wideouts Elroy Hirsch and Tom Fears, made them such fan favorites that in 1950 they became the first NFL team to have all their games televised. Soon enough, the rest of the sports world began to migrate to Southern California: The Dodgers came in 1958, the Chargers of the AFL were founded in 1960, the Lakers moved from Minneapolis in 1960, and the expansion Angels became the second baseball team in town in 1961.

While the Rams would not win a championship in the 1960s or 1970s, they were nonetheless consistently excellent under coach George Allen, who started in 1966, and with the Fearsome Foursome defensive line, the most dominating unit the league had ever seen. Two of those star lineman, Deacon Jones and Merlin Olsen, have their places here, though not without mention of Rosey Grier and Lamar Lundy, who completed the quartet. Jones was an eight-time Pro Bowler and five-time first-team All-Pro, known for popularizing the term *sack* in football. He unofficially recorded over 159.5 sacks during his Rams career, terrorizing quarterbacks with his speed and power off the edge. The *Los Angeles Times* once wrote that Jones was "the most valuable Ram of all time." Alongside him was Olsen, a fourteen-time Pro Bowler and five-time first-team All-Pro, known for his exceptional strength and technique, unofficially tallying 91 sacks. Later generations would come to know Olsen as an actor; he starred on NBC's *Little House on the Prairie* for several seasons, along with other television work. But to football fans, Olsen will always be one of the most dominating defenders of all time.

Kurt Warner's tenure with the St. Louis Rams was arguably the most improbable journey to greatness the league has ever seen, so dramatic that the story was made into a feature film called *American Underdog*. Warner went from working in a grocery store in Iowa to leading the Rams to a championship in Super Bowl XXXIV—in which he earned MVP after throwing for a then-record 414 yards. During his time leading the Greatest Show on Turf, Warner was twice named the league's MVP.

The final face belongs to Aaron Donald, who played all ten of his NFL seasons with the Rams, was named to the Pro Bowl in all ten, and eight times earned First-Team All-Pro honors. In the postseason that resulted in the Rams winning Super Bowl LVI, Donald seemed to make all the biggest plays when they mattered most. He pressured Jimmy Garoppolo into throwing the interception that sealed the NFC championship, and then registered two sacks in the Super Bowl and pressured the quarterback with less than a minute remaining to seal the victory. With no disrespect intended toward Cooper Kupp, who caught two touchdowns in the game, I will always believe that Donald should have been named Super Bowl MVP.

#54
CLEVELAND GUARDIANS

× **Nap Lajoie** ×
× **Bob Feller** ×
× **Larry Doby** ×
× **Jim Thome** ×

For all the passion and loyalty of Cleveland baseball fans (as depicted in the movie *Major League* and in evidence at the ballpark and talk radio every single day of the year), it is difficult to imagine that there was a time when the game was nearly banned in the city—by the city. In 1857, baseball was played in Cleveland's public squares in front of interested spectators nearly every day. City authorities, for reasons known only to them, searched for an ordinance to forbid it. Thankfully, no such law was ever passed or found.

Decades later, when the American League declared itself a major league in 1901, Cleveland was among the eight charter franchises. Two years later, the team name was changed from the Blues to the Naps, in honor of the team's legendary captain, Nap Lajoie. When Lajoie departed for Philadelphia in 1915, the team owner charged the baseball writers with choosing a new name, which is how the Indians came to be, a name that remained in use for more than a century. To the chagrin of the eternally loyal Cleveland fans, no MLB team currently suffers a lengthier championship drought; the city last celebrated a World Series title in 1948, and perhaps no fan base is more deserving of finally seeing that banner raised.

As evidenced by having the franchise literally named in his honor, Lajoie is where this list begins. He played in Cleveland from 1902 to 1914 as a rugged second baseman and .339 career hitter with the team. He collected more hits (2,047) than any player in franchise history.

Bob Feller played all eighteen of his MLB seasons for the Indians, between 1936 and 1956; his career was interrupted by nearly four full years of military service as a naval chief petty officer during World War II. Rapid Robert, as he was known, had the most dominant fastball of his era, resulting in his eight all-star selections, three no-hitters, and leading the American League in strikeouts seven times. Despite missing much of his prime in the war effort, Feller finished with 266 wins, 2,581 strikeouts, and a place in the Baseball Hall of Fame on his first ballot in 1962.

There is no recitation of Larry Doby's statistics—extraordinary though they were—that could begin to do justice to his significance to the history of the franchise or baseball itself. Doby was the first African American player in the American League, following Jackie Robinson's integration of the major leagues by less than three months. Because there was no interleague play, Doby became the first Black player in every stadium he visited, and endured much of the same treatment Robinson did; in fact, Doby was the first player to go directly from the Negro Leagues to the majors. (Robinson played in the minors.) Doby made the leap because he was an outstanding player; a seven-time all-star in Cleveland, he helped lead the Indians to two pennants and a World Series championship in 1948.

Prolific slugger Jim Thome rounds out the group. Playing in Cleveland from 1991 to 2002, Thome hit a franchise-best 337 of his career 612 home runs in the city's uniform. He helped lead Cleveland to six postseason appearances in a seven-year stretch, including World Series berths in 1995 and 1997.

#55
DENVER BRONCOS

⚔ **John Elway** ⚔
⚔ **Terrell Davis** ⚔
⚔ **Von Miller** ⚔
⚔ **Peyton Manning** ⚔

The early days of the Denver Broncos could not have been less auspicious. Simply put, they were the worst team in the American Football League, of which they were a founding member in 1960. Over the decade that ensued before the AFL's merger with the NFL, the Broncos were the only original AFL team to never play in the league championship game or post a single winning season, compiling a 39–97–4 record. The Broncos would finally begin to achieve success during the 1970s, with teams best remembered for the Orange Crush defense, a run that included an appearance in Super Bowl XII.

But it was in 1983 that the fortunes of this franchise would change forever, with the acquisition via trade of quarterback John Elway. It is not far-fetched to suggest that Elway meant as much to the Broncos as any football player has ever meant to any franchise. During his sixteen seasons, Elway was responsible for 334 touchdowns (300 passing, 33 rushing, 1 receiving) and thus generated 4,771 of Denver's 5,806 points scored, more than 82 percent of the total. Prior to Elway's arrival, the Broncos had won a combined total of two playoff games; he led them to fourteen playoff victories, five Super Bowls, and their first two championships. In his final game he threw for 336 yards and was named the MVP of Super Bowl XXXIII, becoming the first Hall of Fame quarterback to finish his career with a Super Bowl win.

Elway's contribution to the Broncos franchise would not end after throwing his final pass. It was Elway who convinced Peyton Manning to join the Broncos upon that quarterback's departure from Indianapolis, a decision that would result in the second golden era of Denver football. Manning would throw 140 touchdowns in his four seasons as a Bronco, winning league MVP in 2013 and displacing Elway as the oldest starting quarterback to win a Super Bowl when the Broncos beat Carolina in Super Bowl 50. While Peyton's most glorious seasons came as a Colt, his tenure in Denver is well worth his place on this list—not only because of the championship, but because of that 2013 season in which he virtually rewrote the NFL record book. During that season, the Broncos broke the scoring record with 606 points, as Manning threw for 5,477 yards and 55 touchdowns. Both records still stand.

The other two members of this quartet earn their places primarily through facilitating titles won by these legendary quarterbacks. Denver's first championship came in Super Bowl XXXII, in an upset of heavily favored

Green Bay. While Elway's "helicopter run" and owner Pat Bowlen's exclamation "This one's for John" remain the most lasting images of the game, running back Terrell Davis was named MVP, rushing for 157 yards and three touchdowns. Davis's career was cut short by injury, but he was well deserving of his Hall of Fame selection. He rushed for 7,607 yards and scored 60 rushing touchdowns in his career, with his most notable season coming in 1998 when he rushed for 2,008 yards and 21 touchdowns, earning NFL MVP honors and his second Offensive Player of the Year award.

Meanwhile, Manning's championship in Denver was largely carried by a dominating defense led by Von Miller, who was named Super Bowl MVP after registering two and a half sacks and forcing two fumbles. While in Denver from 2011 to 2021, Miller was an eight-time Pro Bowler and recorded 110.5 sacks, the most in franchise history.

#56
UTAH JAZZ

For those not aware of the history of the Jazz franchise it is easy to imagine a great deal of confusion over its nickname. Salt Lake City is known for a great many things—jazz music most definitely not among them. The answer, of course, is that the Jazz were born in the home of the blues: the New Orleans Jazz were an expansion team that began play in 1974, an inauspicious beginning that lasted five seasons and moved across the country to Utah. The Jazz played their first season in two New Orleans venues: Municipal Auditorium and Loyola Field House. The issues at Loyola were pronounced; the court was raised so high that the NBA Players Association deemed it unsafe, resulting in the team placing a fishing net around it to prevent players from falling into the stands. Meanwhile, the Jazz were among the least successful teams in the league—it was ten years into their existence before they had their first winning season.

Once the Jazz finally began to play winning ball, they didn't stop for a long time. Utah made the playoffs for the first time in 1984 and would not miss the postseason again until 2004. That success was the direct result of back-to-back first round picks: John Stockton in 1984 and Karl Malone in 1985. The two would go on to play more games as teammates than any duo in NBA history, leading the Jazz to back-to-back NBA Finals appearances in 1997 and 1998, where they fell in epic battles to Michael Jordan's Bulls both times.

Stockton and Malone are, of course, forever faces of the franchise. Stockton played more games for Utah (1,686, including playoffs) than any player for any team in NBA history. He played all nineteen of his seasons for the Jazz, retiring as the league's all-time leader in both assists and steals. Remarkably, during his nineteen seasons, he would play in all eighty-two games a record sixteen times, make eleven All-NBA teams, and lead his teams to the playoffs in every season of his career from the age of twenty-three through age forty-one. Malone, known as the Mailman, played eighteen seasons for Utah, winning two league MVP Awards and earning fourteen All-NBA selections. Malone would average 25.4 points and 10.2 rebounds during his Jazz career, retiring as the second all-time leading scorer in league history.

Jerry Sloan was the coach for most of that legendary run, taking the helm after his long career as a hard-nosed guard, primarily for Chicago. As coach, Sloan led the Jazz to nineteen playoff appearances in twenty-three seasons and two Finals appearances. He was inducted into the Hall of Fame in 2009 and retired from coaching two years later.

The final face of the franchise is actually its first: Pete Maravich, one of the most dynamic and beloved players in league history. Pistol Pete played for the Jazz from 1974 to 1979, demonstrating unforgettable ball-handling, flashy passing, and outstanding deep shooting in an era before the three-point line. Maravich made three All-NBA teams during his tenure with the Jazz, averaging 25.2 points, including a league-high 31.1 in 1976–77.

#57
ST. LOUIS BLUES

× **Bernie Federko** ×
× **Brian Sutter** ×
× **Brett Hull** ×
× **Chris Pronger** ×

William Christopher Handy was a legendary com-
poser and musician who was widely known as the
Father of the Blues. His most famous song (among the
genre's first songs to achieve popular success) was 1914's
"Saint Louis Blues." The song remains fundamental to the
history of jazz, and has been recorded by Louis Armstrong,
Cab Calloway, Guy Lombardo, Count Basie, and Glenn
Miller, among many others; so seminal is the song that it
is sometimes called "the jazzman's *Hamlet*." Thus, in 1967,
when the NHL expanded from the Original Six to twelve
teams, the franchise based in St. Louis took its name from
that iconic song.

In the early stages of their history, the Blues made regular visits to the postseason, including trips to the Stanley
Cup Final in each of their first three seasons. All of those
ended in frustration, as did every playoff journey the franchise would undertake for the first fifty-two years of its
history. Then, in 2019, forty-nine years removed from
their last visit to the championship round, the Blues lifted

the Cup and became the last active team from the 1967 expansion to finally win it all.

Bernie Federko, a center known for his playmaking ability and vision, played all but one of his fourteen NHL seasons in St. Louis. Federko's hallmark was his consistency: He became the first NHL player ever to record at least fifty assists in ten consecutive seasons. He remains the all-time franchise leader in career assists (721) and points (1,073); his number 24 was retired the year after he finished his career. He was inducted into the Hall of Fame in 2002, the first player to be inducted largely based on his achievements as a Blue.

Brian Sutter was a left wing and nine-season team captain in St. Louis, renowned for his grit and tenacity, and totaled 636 points in 779 games with the Blues. Sutter played a crucial leadership role in the team's playoff runs in the 1980s. Immediately after retiring, Sutter was named the Blues' head coach, winning the Jack Adams Award as Coach of the Year in 1991; in all, Sutter spent sixteen consecutive years at ice level with the Blues. Brian is the oldest of the legendary Sutter brothers to play in the NHL and had his number 11 retired in 1988.

Brett Hull was one of the greatest goal scorers in NHL history and will always be best remembered for his time in St. Louis, from 1988 to 1998. The son of hockey icon Bobby Hull, Brett was known for his lethal shot, scoring 741 career goals, with 527 of those coming as a Blue, making him the franchise's all-time leading goal scorer. Hull led the NHL in goals in three consecutive seasons from 1989 to 1992, the second of which yielded him the league MVP award.

Hall of Fame defenseman Chris Pronger was a dominant force for the Blues from 1995 to 2004. Known for his imposing physical presence, Pronger is only one of two players in history to win both the Norris Trophy as the league's best defenseman and the Hart Memorial Trophy as the league MVP. The Blues retired Pronger's number 44 in 2022.

#58
BALTIMORE ORIOLES

⚔ **Brooks Robinson** ⚔
⚔ **Jim Palmer** ⚔
⚔ **Earl Weaver** ⚔
⚔ **Cal Ripken Jr.** ⚔

It is a little-known but fascinating note that the Baltimore Orioles were actually the Milwaukee Brewers long before the current Brewers were. That franchise was one of eight charter teams of the American League in 1901, playing one season in Milwaukee as the Brewers before departing for St. Louis, where they competed as the Browns for fifty-two years. Baseball would return to Milwaukee when the Boston Braves moved in 1953, then moved again to Atlanta in 1966. The Brewers as we know them came to Milwaukee in 1970 after a single season as the Seattle Pilots. It's a lot to keep track of, to be sure, but a fascinating glimpse into the transient nature of the sport's history—not to mention, a decent way to win a bar bet tonight if you are so inclined.

As for the Orioles, they arrived in Baltimore in 1954 and went on to make six World Series appearances from 1966 to 1983, winning three. They were the last remaining charter member of the AL to win a pennant, and then the last to win a championship.

The first icon of Baltimore baseball was Brooks Robinson, the Hall of Fame third baseman, sixteen-time Gold Glove winner and 1964 AL MVP. Known for his exceptional defensive skills, he revolutionized play at third base while adding 2,848 hits and 268 home runs. Robinson won two World Series titles with the Orioles and was named the 1970 World Series MVP, batting .429 and showcasing some of the greatest defense in the history of the fall classic.

The ace of the Baltimore staff during their championship era was Jim Palmer, six-time all-star, four-time Gold Glove winner, and three-time Cy Young Award winner. He won three championships with the Orioles and logged a 2.61 ERA across 124.1 postseason innings. Known for his consistency, Palmer recorded 268 wins, 2,212 strikeouts, and a career 2.86 ERA. Inducted into the Hall of Fame in 1990, Palmer has remained intimately connected with the Orioles as a broadcaster since his retirement as a player.

Earl Weaver, the Orioles manager from 1968 to 1982, and then again from 1985 to 1986, was a fiery and strategic skipper known for both his analytical approach and his legendary confrontations with umpires. Weaver guided the Orioles to six division titles and four pennants, won the World Series in 1970, and was inducted into the Hall of Fame in 1996.

Baltimore's greatest player, and greatest legend, was— and remains—Cal Ripken Jr., among the most decorated and admired players in the game's history. Ripken was a nineteen-time all-star and two-time AL MVP, but will be best remembered for his unmatched durability: He broke Lou Gehrig's Iron Man streak by playing in 2,632 consecutive games, a record that seems highly unlikely to ever be broken. Ripken played shortstop and third base during his career and finished with 3,184 hits and 431 home runs.

#59
LOS ANGELES KINGS

× Marcel Dionne ×
× Wayne Gretzky ×
× Anže Kopitar ×
× Jonathan Quick ×

When the National Hockey League doubled in size in 1967 by adding six expansion teams, one of the new owners was the legendary Canadian entrepreneur Jack Kent Cooke, who paid two million dollars to begin a franchise in Los Angeles. Always prone to a flourish, Cooke named the team the Kings and chose team colors purple and gold to attach an air of royalty to his new franchise. Shortly thereafter, Cooke would also adapt those colors for the basketball team he owned, the Los Angeles Lakers.

The early history of the franchise can generally be divided into two eras: before and after the acquisition of Wayne Gretzky in 1988. Until then, the Kings had had several good seasons, finishing in the top two of their division six times between 1968 and 1981, but their post-seasons were generally marked by disappointment, and they won just four playoff series before Gretzky arrived. And then came August 9, 1988, and one of the most famous (or infamous, depending on your perspective) trades in sports history. While Gretzky would not ultimately bring a championship to LA (the Great One–led Kings would make their first Stanley Cup Final appearance in 1993 but lose to the Canadiens) his star power and allure elevated the profile of the team and the entire league. The team's breakthrough would come two decades later, under coach Darryl Sutter, as the Kings would finally raise the Cup, first in 2012 and then again two years later. Still, Gretzky deserves a space here for the eight seasons he played with LA, bringing an electricity to Hollywood that the franchise may have never achieved otherwise. He led the NHL in scoring in three of those seasons and tallied 40 points across 24 playoff games in 1993.

The first true legend of West Coast hockey was Marcel Dionne, who arrived in Los Angeles in 1975. Known both for his exceptional scoring ability and playmaking, Dionne finished top five in MVP voting with the Kings four times between 1977 and 1981; he totaled 1,307 points in 921 games with the team, which remains the all-time franchise scoring record.

Anže Kopitar was the star center when the Kings broke through for their two Stanley Cups. Known for exceptional two-way play and leadership, Kopitar is a two-time recipient of the Frank J. Selke Trophy, given annually to the NHL's top defensive forward. He is the all-time franchise leader in assists and second behind Dionne in points.

Goaltender Jonathan Quick was the defensive backbone of the championship teams, known for his acrobatic

saves and exceptional reflexes. He won the Conn Smythe
Trophy as playoff MVP in 2012 to cap the Kings' first title
run with a .946 save percentage and three shutouts. Quick
ranks as the franchise leader in career games in goal, as
well as most wins and most shutouts.

#60
PHOENIX SUNS

× **Paul Westphal** ×
× **Charles Barkley** ×
× **Steve Nash** ×
× **Devin Booker** ×

The Suns were the first major professional sports team in Phoenix and are the only one that uses the city as their identifier, given that the NFL's Cardinals and MLB's Diamondbacks represent the entire state. The Suns and Bucks joined the NBA together in 1968 and would flip a coin the following year to determine who would receive the first pick in the draft. The Bucks won and selected Lew Alcindor—sometimes history is entirely dependent on the toss of a coin. While Milwaukee would win an NBA title with Alcindor, the Suns are still searching for their elusive first championship.

The franchise has made three trips to the Finals, each ending in frustration. The first, in 1976, was among the most surprising playoff runs in league history: After finishing 42–40, the Suns ended a playoff drought, knocked out Seattle in six games, stunned the defending champion Warriors in seven, and then lost in the Finals to the Celtics in a series that featured a triple-overtime thriller in Game 5. A generation later, league MVP Charles Barkley would lead the Suns back to the Finals in 1993, where they would play another triple-overtime marathon in Chicago (those remain the only triple-overtime games in NBA Finals history) before eventually succumbing to Michael Jordan's Bulls in six games. The third Finals appearance for Phoenix was perhaps the most disappointing: In 2021 the Suns jumped to a two-games-to-none lead over the Bucks before losing the next four, with Giannis Antetokounmpo pouring in fifty points in the Game 6 clincher.

Among the few common threads of the Suns' best teams was Paul Westphal, who starred as their point guard in the 1970s—including the magic run in 1976—and then coached the team back to the championship round in '93. In total, Westphal played six seasons in Phoenix, and was All-NBA in four of them.

Steve Nash played for the Suns from 1996 to 1998 and 2004 to 2012, transforming the team with his exceptional playmaking and shooting at the center of the Seven Seconds or Less offense, emphasizing rapid ball movement and scoring. He won consecutive MVP awards in 2005 and 2006, leading Phoenix to the Western Conference Finals in both seasons.

Devin Booker joined the Suns in 2015 as the thirteenth overall pick in the draft and quickly emerged as the team's cornerstone and one of the most dynamic new stars in the sport. In 2017, Booker became the youngest player to score 70 points in a game (20 years, 145 days old). In his first-ever postseason, Booker averaged over 27 points in a run that ended in the Finals.

The final space here is reserved for Al McCoy, the forever voice of the Suns, and the longest tenured broadcaster in NBA history. McCoy began calling games for the franchise in 1972 and remained through 2023; he was honored by the Naismith Hall of Fame in 2007 as the seventeenth electronic media recipient of the Curt Gowdy Media Award. Longtime Suns owner Jerry Colangelo said of the legendary announcer, "[He was] the greatest salesman for the game of basketball in our entire state, who had as much to do with the success of the Suns as any player, coach, or manager."

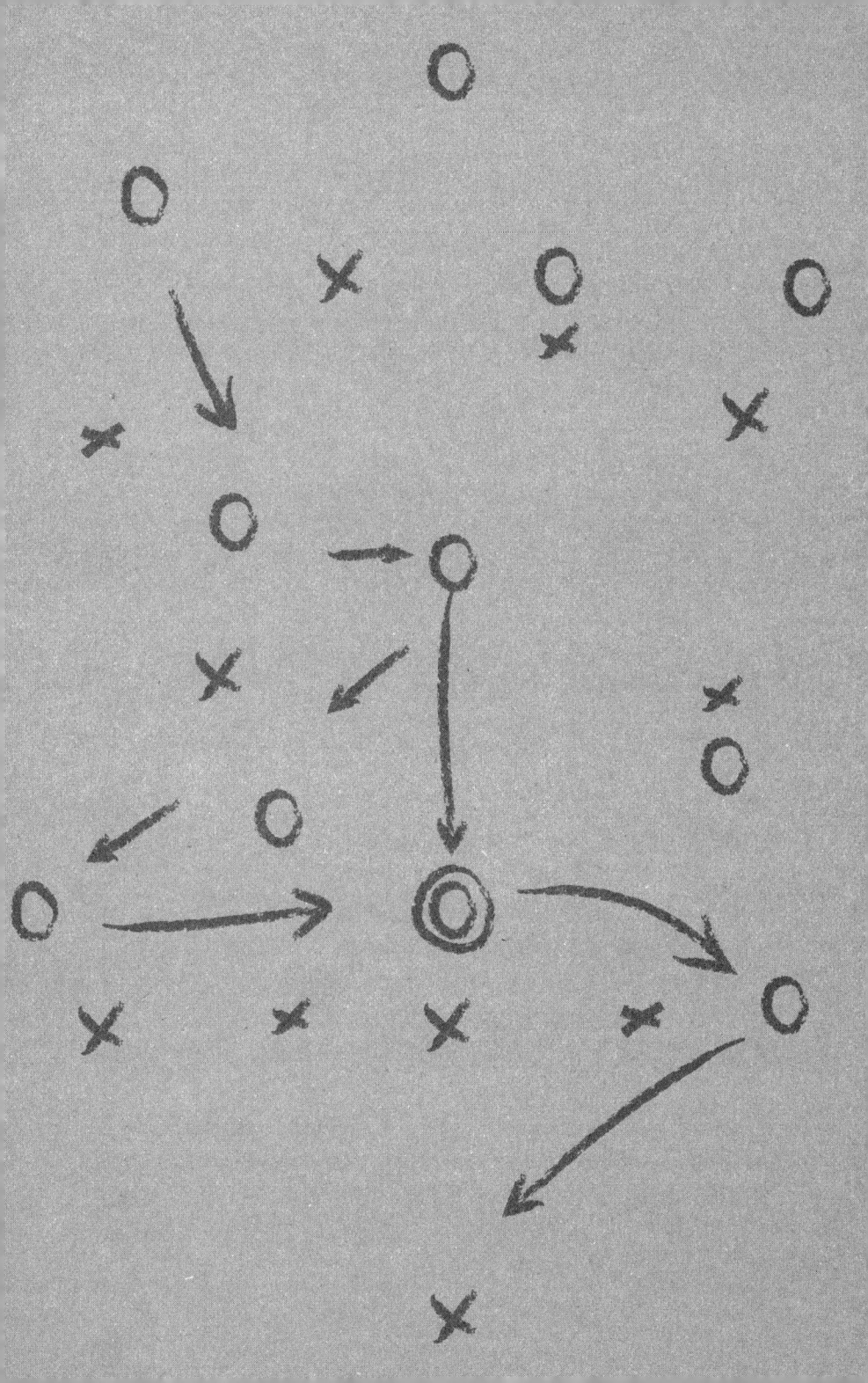

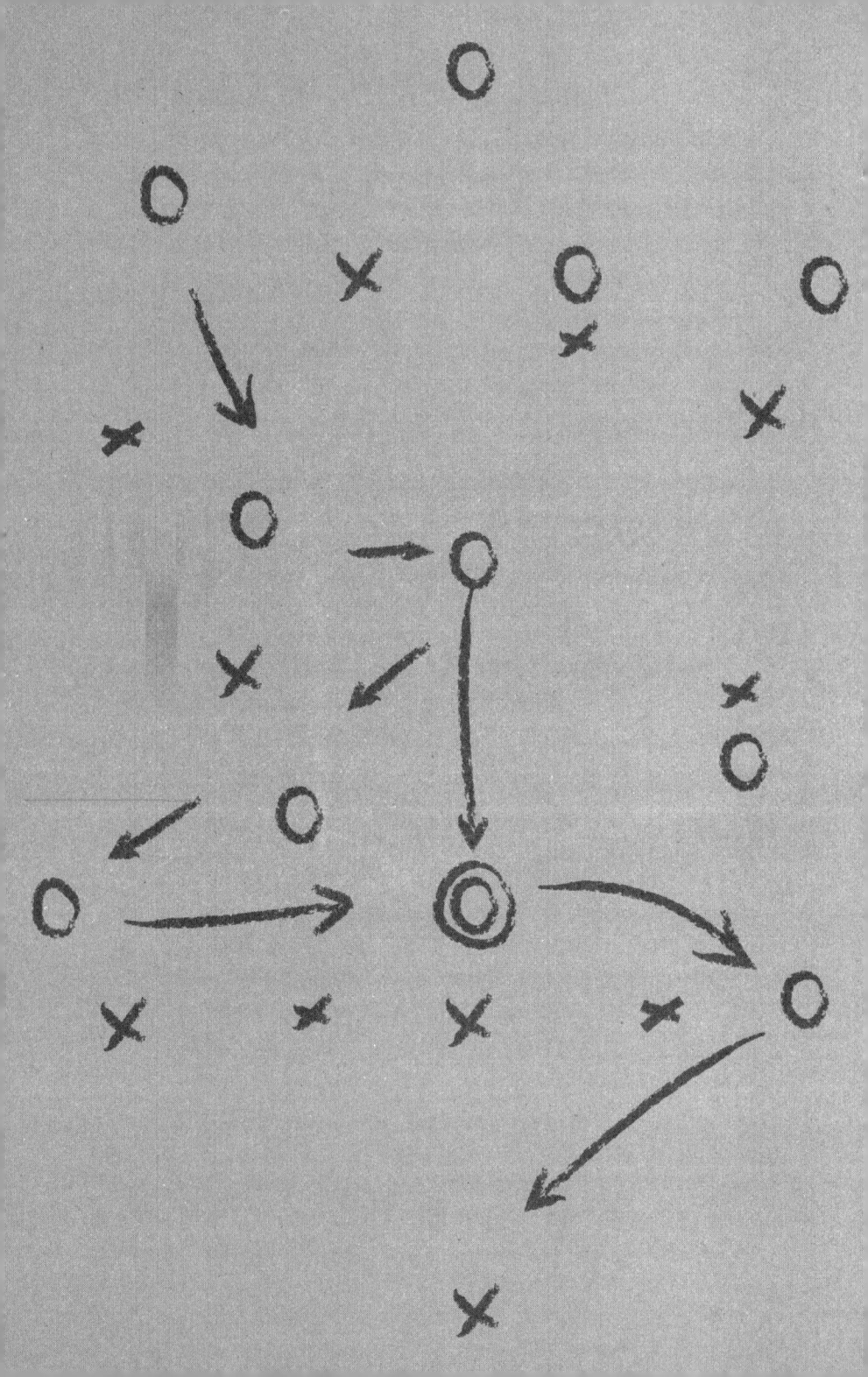

OUTRO

I n case it does not go without saying, this book is designed to be a living document, meaning that if we had written it ten years ago any number of things would have been different, and there is no doubt the same will be true ten years from now. That is the fundamental beauty of sports: In each day, each game, each season, there is the possibility that history will be rewritten.

A book like this is meant to celebrate the greatness that is achieved in each of those days, games, and seasons, the feats that inspire us, the passion that consumes us, and those precious, fleeting moments wherein watching a human being play a game can quite literally take our breath away. The selection of franchise legends was the more enjoyable piece of this exercise, and while no shortage of research, data, and study went into the decisions, the guiding principle was actually quite simple: *When you close your eyes and think of a franchise, who is it that comes to mind?*

The first four answers to that question, nine times out of ten, are the right choices to represent the organization as a whole. After all, a sporting franchise is unlike most other businesses I can think of in that the sum of its parts is not nearly as important as the individuals who created it. For example, the Yankees are not the Yankees because they represent New York, or because of their iconic logo, or even because of all the World Series they've won. All of these things are the results, not the origin. The Yankees are the Yankees because Babe Ruth played for them—and Lou Gehrig, and all the rest—and because of everything those people did and all the ways they made others feel.

If you don't believe that, consider how much you know of Ruth's life and career, and then let it sink in that he played his final game in the same month that Amelia Earhart flew from Mexico City to Newark, New Jersey, in a record 14 hours, 22 minutes, and 50 seconds, becoming the first pilot to fly that route without stopping along the way. A quick internet search suggests that, as I sit here now, there is a seemingly unlimited supply of daily flights on that route, most with an estimated duration of four hours and thirty minutes. The point, in case it isn't clear, is that Babe Ruth was a baseball player—he played a game for a living—and today he is infinitely better remembered than a contemporary who fundamentally changed the world as we know it.

Or maybe the lesson in that really is that Ruth changed the world, too. Just as everyone in this book did. Sports change the world pretty much every day, usually in the best possible ways.

Much less esoteric was the selection of the tiers in

which the teams would be placed; if the first process was an art, this one was a science. (When it comes to measuring the success of a franchise, actual *measuring* is the only thing you need to do.) The sole decisions required of us were choosing criteria, which we did with these two as our guiding principles:

1. Nothing is more important than championships.
2. A high floor is more valuable than an impressive ceiling.

The first point pretty much speaks for itself. The second, obviously, requires an explanation. Simply put, it seems to me there are multiple ways to be a .500 team over the course of, say, a decade. One of them is to win half your games every single year, another might be winning 80 percent of your games in two seasons while being the worst team in the league the other eight. Assuming in both cases there is no championship-round appearance, then the more consistent winner deserves the nod; there is something to be said for never being awful. Thus were the decisions regarding ranking the teams made fairly easily, with the human element required only to break a few ties along the way.

In closing, we hope you enjoyed this stroll through the entire history of North American sports as much as we did. And, as always, should anyone ask why this stuff matters so much, simply tell them: *Because there is nothing in the world better than investing everything into things that mean absolutely nothing.*

Long live sports, forever.

—Greeny

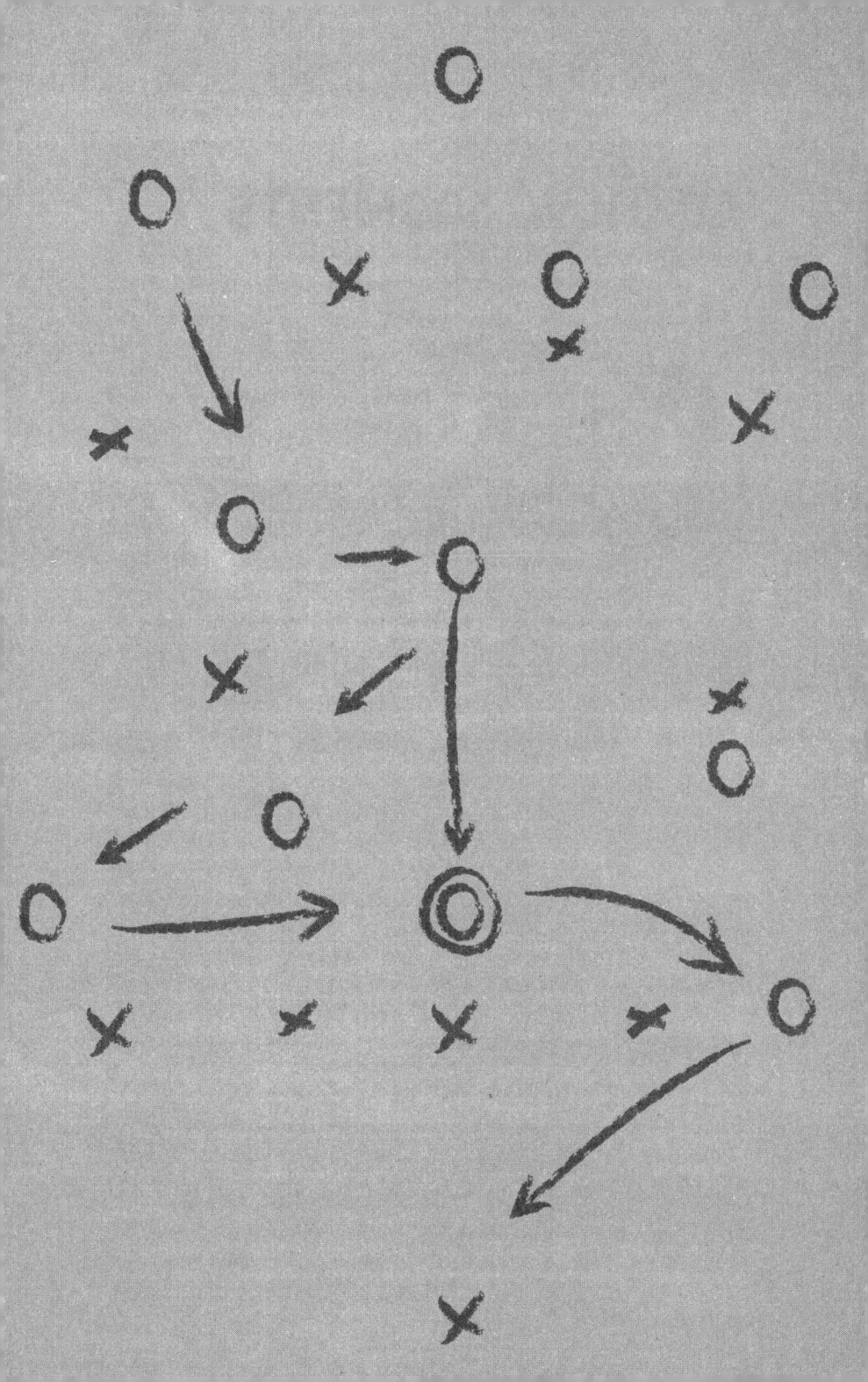

ACKNOWLEDGMENTS

Endless thanks to Team Greeny: David Larabell and my entire squad at CAA, Mark and Jason Bradburn at Morgan Stanley, Richard Koenigsberg at Eisner Amper, Nick Khan, and Erika Echavarria. Thanks to the outstanding, dedicated teams I have the privilege of working with at ESPN every day. And, most of all, thanks to every one of you who chooses to start your morning with me. It has truly been the ride of a lifetime.

—Greeny

ACKNOWLEDGMENTS

Thank you. To my extraordinary wife, Lizzie, for encouraging me to pursue my dreams. To Greg Thompson and Tom Johnstone, for your inspiration, our shared fandom, and your friendship. To Greeny, for your daily investment to my career. And to all those who read, listen, and watch, for the unending support.

—Hembo

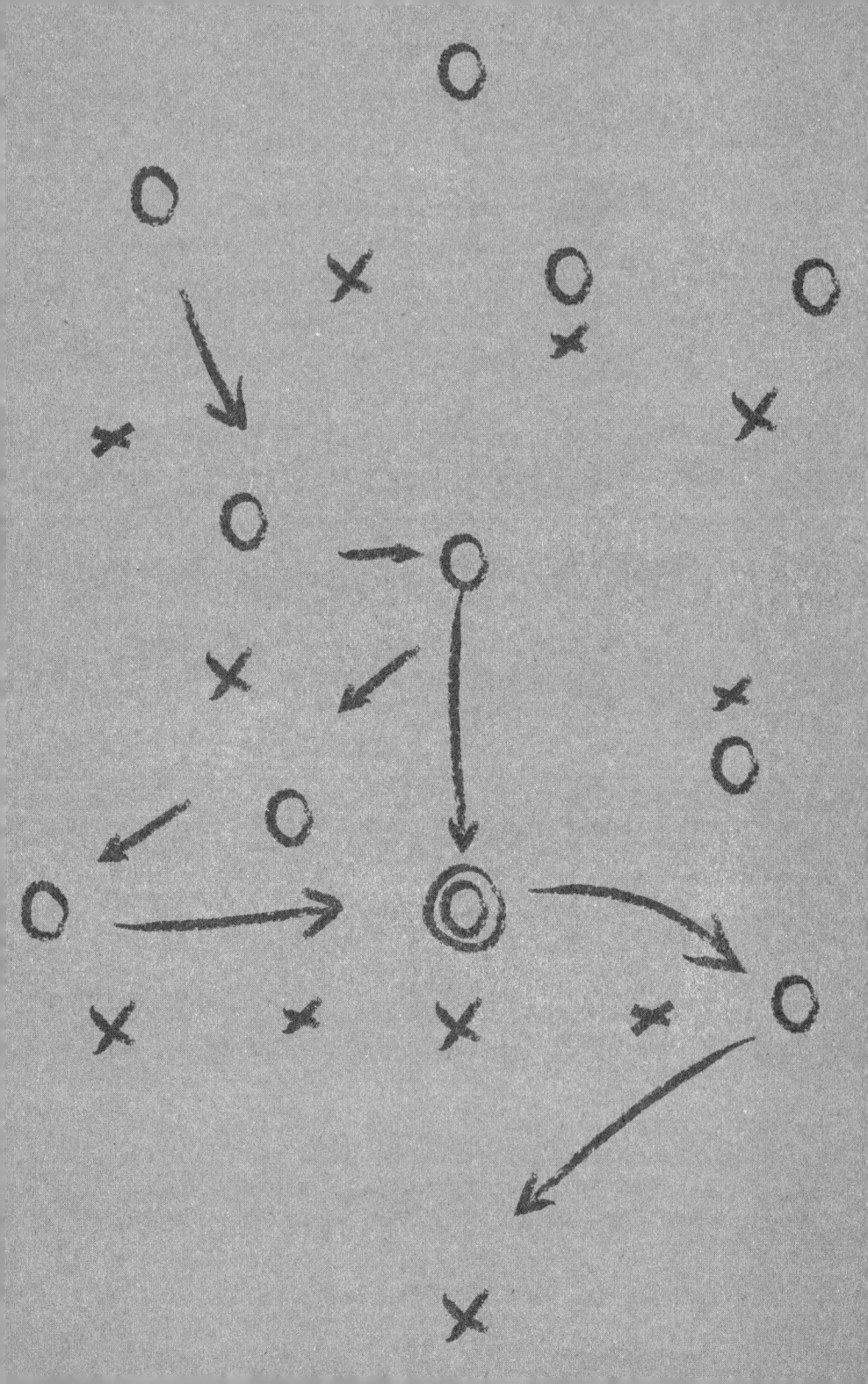

THE MOUNT RUSHMORES OF LEGENDS

1	**YANKEES**			BASEBALL
	Babe Ruth	Lou Gehrig	Joe DiMaggio	Mickey Mantle

2	**CELTICS**			BASKETBALL
	Red Auerbach	Bill Russell	John Havlicek	Larry Bird

3	**CANADIENS**			HOCKEY
	Maurice Richard	Jean Béliveau	Jacques Plante	Guy Lafleur

4	**PACKERS**			FOOTBALL
	Vince Lombardi	Bart Starr	Brett Favre	Aaron Rodgers

5	**LAKERS**			BASKETBALL
	Jerry West	Kareem Abdul-Jabbar	Magic Johnson	Kobe Bryant

6 — RED WINGS — HOCKEY

| Gordie Howe | Terry Sawchuk | Nicklas Lidström | Steve Yzerman |

7 — CARDINALS [MLB] — BASEBALL

| Stan Musial | Bob Gibson | Ozzie Smith | Albert Pujols |

8 — STEELERS — FOOTBALL

| Chuck Noll | Joe Greene | Terry Bradshaw | Franco Harris |

9 — GIANTS [MLB] — BASEBALL

| Christy Mathewson | John McGraw | Willie Mays | Barry Bonds |

10 — PATRIOTS — FOOTBALL

| John Hannah | Bill Belichick | Tom Brady | Rob Gronkowski |

11 — OILERS — HOCKEY

| Wayne Gretzky | Mark Messier | Grant Fuhr | Connor McDavid |

12 — BULLS — BASKETBALL

| Jerry Krause | Michael Jordan | Phil Jackson | Scottie Pippen |

13 DODGERS — BASEBALL

Jackie Robinson	Vin Scully	Sandy Koufax	Clayton Kershaw

14 SPURS — BASKETBALL

George Gervin	Gregg Popovich	David Robinson	Tim Duncan

15 COWBOYS — FOOTBALL

Tom Landry	Roger Staubach	Jerry Jones	Emmitt Smith

16 49ERS — FOOTBALL

Bill Walsh	Joe Montana	Ronnie Lott	Jerry Rice

17 PENGUINS — HOCKEY

Mario Lemieux	Jaromír Jágr	Sidney Crosby	Evgeni Malkin

18 BRUINS — HOCKEY

Eddie Shore	Bobby Orr	Phil Esposito	Ray Bourque

19 BEARS — FOOTBALL

George Halas	Mike Ditka	Dick Butkus	Walter Payton

20 GIANTS [NFL]

FOOTBALL

| Frank Gifford | Lawrence Taylor | Michael Strahan | Eli Manning |

21 RED SOX

BASEBALL

| Ted Williams | Carl Yastrzemski | Pedro Martínez | David Ortiz |

22 WARRIORS

BASKETBALL

| Wilt Chamberlain | Rick Barry | Stephen Curry | Draymond Green |

23 ATHLETICS

BASEBALL

| Connie Mack | Jimmie Foxx | Reggie Jackson | Rickey Henderson |

24 MAPLE LEAFS

HOCKEY

| Turk Broda | Tim Horton | Darryl Sittler | Mats Sundin |

25 76ERS

BASKETBALL

| Dolph Schayes | Julius Erving | Allen Iverson | Joel Embiid |

26 REDS

BASEBALL

| Pete Rose | Johnny Bench | Joe Morgan | Barry Larkin |

27 · ISLANDERS — HOCKEY

Billy Smith	Denis Potvin	Bryan Trottier	Mike Bossy

28 · HEAT — BASKETBALL

Pat Riley	Alonzo Mourning	Dwyane Wade	LeBron James

29 · BROWNS — FOOTBALL

Paul Brown	Otto Graham	Jim Brown	Joe Thomas

30 · BLACKHAWKS — HOCKEY

Bobby Hull	Stan Mikita	Patrick Kane	Jonathan Toews

31 · CHIEFS — FOOTBALL

Len Dawson	Derrick Thomas	Travis Kelce	Patrick Mahomes

32 · PIRATES — BASEBALL

Honus Wagner	Roberto Clemente	Bill Mazeroski	Willie Stargell

33 · RANGERS [NHL] — HOCKEY

Rod Gilbert	Brian Leetch	Mark Messier	Henrik Lundqvist

34 BRAVES — BASEBALL

| Warren Spahn | Hank Aaron | Greg Maddux | Chipper Jones |

35 TIGERS — BASEBALL

| Ty Cobb | Hank Greenberg | Al Kaline | Miguel Cabrera |

36 AVALANCHE — HOCKEY

| Peter Šťastný | Joe Sakic | Peter Forsberg | Patrick Roy |

37 PISTONS — BASKETBALL

| Bob Lanier | Isiah Thomas | Joe Dumars | Chauncey Billups |

38 RAVENS — FOOTBALL

| Jonathan Ogden | Ray Lewis | Ed Reed | Lamar Jackson |

39 BUCKS — BASKETBALL

| Kareem Abdul-Jabbar | Jon McGlocklin | Sidney Moncrief | Giannis Antetokounmpo |

40 KNICKERBOCKERS — BASKETBALL

| Marv Albert | Willis Reed | Walt Frazier | Patrick Ewing |

41 COLTS — FOOTBALL

Gino Marchetti	Johnny Unitas	Marvin Harrison	Peyton Manning

42 CUBS — BASEBALL

Ernie Banks	Ron Santo	Harry Caray	Ryne Sandberg

43 WHITE SOX — BASEBALL

Shoeless Joe Jackson	Nellie Fox	Ken "Hawk" Harrelson	Frank Thomas

44 ROCKETS — BASKETBALL

Rudy Tomjanovich	Moses Malone	Hakeem Olajuwon	James Harden

45 LIGHTNING — HOCKEY

Vincent Lecavalier	Martin St. Louis	Steven Stamkos	Nikita Kucherov

46 COMMANDERS — FOOTBALL

Sammy Baugh	Jack Kent Cooke	Joe Gibbs	Darrell Green

47 DEVILS — HOCKEY

Lou Lamoriello	Martin Brodeur	Scott Stevens	Patrik Eliáš

48

THUNDER
BASKETBALL

| Jack Sikma | Gary Payton | Kevin Durant | Russell Westbrook |

49

TWINS
BASEBALL

| Walter Johnson | Harmon Killebrew | Rod Carew | Kirby Puckett |

50

EAGLES
FOOTBALL

| Chuck Bednarik | Reggie White | Brian Dawkins | Jason Kelce |

51

FLYERS
HOCKEY

| Bernie Parent | Bobby Clarke | Eric Lindros | Claude Giroux |

52

NUGGETS
BASKETBALL

| Dan Issel | Alex English | Carmelo Anthony | Nikola Jokić |

53

RAMS
FOOTBALL

| Deacon Jones | Merlin Olsen | Kurt Warner | Aaron Donald |

54

GUARDIANS
BASEBALL

| Nap Lajoie | Bob Feller | Larry Doby | Jim Thome |

55 — BRONCOS · FOOTBALL

John Elway	Terrell Davis	Von Miller	Peyton Manning

56 — JAZZ · BASKETBALL

Pete Maravich	Jerry Sloan	John Stockton	Karl Malone

57 — BLUES · HOCKEY

Bernie Federko	Brian Sutter	Brett Hull	Chris Pronger

58 — ORIOLES · BASEBALL

Brooks Robinson	Jim Palmer	Earl Weaver	Cal Ripken Jr.

59 — KINGS (NHL) · HOCKEY

Marcel Dionne	Wayne Gretzky	Anže Kopitar	Jonathan Quick

60 — SUNS · BASKETBALL

Paul Westphal	Charles Barkley	Steve Nash	Devin Booker

61 — ASTROS · BASEBALL

Larry Dierker	Craig Biggio	Jeff Bagwell	Jose Altuve

62 DOLPHINS — FOOTBALL

| Don Shula | Brian Griese | Dan Marino | Jason Taylor |

63 TRAIL BLAZERS — BASKETBALL

| Jack Ramsay | Bill Walton | Clyde Drexler | Damian Lillard |

64 FLAMES — HOCKEY

| Al MacInnis | Mike Vernon | Theo Fleury | Jarome Iginla |

65 RAIDERS — FOOTBALL

| Al Davis | Art Shell | Ken Stabler | Marcus Allen |

66 BLUE JAYS — BASEBALL

| Cito Gaston | Joe Carter | Roy Halladay | José Bautista |

67 PACERS — BASKETBALL

| Slick Leonard | George McGinnis | Mel Daniels | Reggie Miller |

68 STARS — HOCKEY

| Neal Broten | Mike Modano | Sergei Zubov | Jamie Benn |

69 — VIKINGS — FOOTBALL

| Fran Tarkenton | Alan Page | Randy Moss | Adrian Peterson |

70 — DUCKS — HOCKEY

| Teemu Selänne | Paul Kariya | Jean-Sébastian Giguère | Ryan Getzlaf |

71 — METS — BASEBALL

| Tom Seaver | Keith Hernandez | Dwight Gooden | Mike Piazza |

72 — MAVERICKS — BASKETBALL

| Rolando Blackman | Dirk Nowitzki | Mark Cuban | Luka Dončić |

73 — SEAHAWKS — FOOTBALL

| Steve Largent | Pete Carroll | Richard Sherman | Russell Wilson |

74 — PHILLIES — BASEBALL

| Richie Ashburn | Mike Schmidt | Steve Carlton | Jimmy Rollins |

75 — CAPITALS — HOCKEY

| Rod Langway | Peter Bondra | Alex Ovechkin | Nicklas Bäckström |

76 NETS — BASKETBALL

| Julius Erving | Buck Williams | Jason Kidd | Richard Jefferson |

77 ROYALS — BASEBALL

| Frank White | George Brett | Bret Saberhagen | Salvador Pérez |

78 LIONS — FOOTBALL

| Bobby Layne | Joe Schmidt | Barry Sanders | Calvin Johnson |

79 HAWKS — BASKETBALL

| Bob Pettit | Lenny Wilkens | Ted Turner | Dominique Wilkins |

80 CANUCKS — HOCKEY

| Trevor Linden | Pavel Bure | Henrik Sedin | Daniel Sedin |

81 CHARGERS — FOOTBALL

| Lance Alworth | Dan Fouts | Junior Seau | LaDainian Tomlinson |

82 ANGELS — BASEBALL

| Nolan Ryan | Chuck Finley | Mike Trout | Shohei Ohtani |

83 CAVALIERS — BASKETBALL

| Mark Price | Brad Daugherty | LeBron James | Kyrie Irving |

84 TITANS — FOOTBALL

| Earl Campbell | Bruce Matthews | Warren Moon | Derrick Henry |

85 SABRES — HOCKEY

| Gilbert Perrault | Rick Martin | Dave Andreychuk | Dominik Hasek |

86 KINGS (NBA) — BASKETBALL

| Jack Twyman | Oscar Robertson | Tiny Archibald | Chris Webber |

87 MARLINS — BASEBALL

| Luis Castillo | Josh Beckett | Giancarlo Stanton | José Fernández |

88 HURRICANES — HOCKEY

| Ron Francis | Rod Brind'Amour | Eric Staal | Cam Ward |

89 BILLS — FOOTBALL

| O. J. Simpson | Bruce Smith | Jim Kelly | Josh Allen |

90 RAPTORS — BASKETBALL

| Vince Carter | DeMar DeRozan | Kyle Lowry | Kawhi Leonard |

91 DIAMONDBACKS — BASEBALL

| Luis Gonzalez | Randy Johnson | Curt Schilling | Paul Goldschmidt |

92 PREDATORS — HOCKEY

| David Legwand | Pekka Rinne | Shea Weber | Roman Josi |

93 BUCCANEERS — FOOTBALL

| Lee Roy Selmon | Warren Sapp | Derrick Brooks | Tom Brady |

94 WIZARDS — BASKETBALL

| Walt Bellamy | Wes Unseld | Elvin Hayes | Gilbert Arenas |

95 PANTHERS (NHL) — HOCKEY

| Scott Mellanby | Pavel Bure | Roberto Luongo | Aleksander Barkov |

96 RAYS — BASEBALL

| Carl Crawford | Evan Longoria | David Price | Randy Arozarena |

97 — SAINTS — FOOTBALL

| Archie Manning | Rickey Jackson | Sean Payton | Drew Brees |

98 — NATIONALS — BASEBALL

| Gary Carter | Tim Raines | Vladimir Guerrero | Ryan Zimmerman |

99 — SENATORS — HOCKEY

| Daniel Alfredsson | Wade Redden | Jason Spezza | Erik Karlsson |

100 — JETS (NFL) — FOOTBALL

| Don Maynard | Joe Namath | Joe Klecko | Darrelle Revis |

101 — RANGERS (MLB) — BASEBALL

| Nolan Ryan | Juan González | Iván Rodriguez | Adrián Beltré |

102 — MAGIC — BASKETBALL

| Shaquille O'Neal | Penny Hardaway | Tracy McGrady | Dwight Howard |

103 — CARDINALS (NFL) — FOOTBALL

| Charley Trippi | Larry Wilson | Dan Dierdorf | Larry Fitzgerald |

104 JETS (NHL)
HOCKEY

| Ilya Kovalchuk | Dustin Byfuglien | Blake Wheeler | Connor Hellebuyck |

105 BREWERS
BASEBALL

| Bud Selig | Bob Uecker | Robin Yount | Paul Molitor |

106 GRIZZLIES
BASKETBALL

| Mike Conley | Marc Gasol | Zach Randolph | Ja Morant |

107 BENGALS
FOOTBALL

| Paul Brown | Anthony Muñoz | Chad Johnson | Joe Burrow |

108 SHARKS
HOCKEY

| Patrick Marleau | Joe Thornton | Joe Pavelski | Brent Burns |

109 CLIPPERS
BASKETBALL

| Bob McAdoo | Elgin Baylor | Blake Griffin | Chris Paul |

110 PANTHERS (NFL)
FOOTBALL

| Steve Smith Sr. | Julius Peppers | Cam Newton | Luke Kuechly |

111

GOLDEN KNIGHTS
HOCKEY

| Marc-André Fleury | Jonathan Marchessault | William Karlsson | Jack Eichel |

112

MARINERS
BASEBALL

| Edgar Martinez | Ken Griffey Jr. | Ichiro Suzuki | Félix Hernández |

113

FALCONS
FOOTBALL

| Tommy Nobis | Deion Sanders | Michael Vick | Matt Ryan |

114

WILD
HOCKEY

| Marián Gáborik | Mikko Koivu | Ryan Suter | Kirill Kaprizov |

115

TIMBERWOLVES
BASKETBALL

| Flip Saunders | Kevin Garnett | Kevin Love | Anthony Edwards |

116

COYOTES
HOCKEY

| Dale Hawerchuk | Teppo Numminen | Keith Tkachuk | Shane Doan |

117

PADRES
BASEBALL

| Dave Winfield | Tony Gwynn | Trevor Hoffman | Manny Machado |

118

TEXANS
FOOTBALL

| Andre Johnson | Arian Foster | J. J. Watt | DeAndre Hopkins |

119

BLUE JACKETS
HOCKEY

| Rick Nash | Cam Atkinson | Sergei Bobrovsky | Nick Foligno |

120

JAGUARS
FOOTBALL

| Tom Coughlin | Jimmy Smith | Tony Boselli | Fred Taylor |

121

PELICANS
BASKETBALL

| David West | Chris Paul | Anthony Davis | Zion Williamson |

122

ROCKIES
BASEBALL

| Larry Walker | Todd Helton | Troy Tulowitzki | Nolan Arenado |

123

HORNETS
BASKETBALL

| Muggsy Bogues | Dell Curry | Michael Jordan | Kemba Walker |

124

KRAKEN
HOCKEY

| Jared McCann | Vince Dunn | Matty Beniers | Adam Larsson |

Sports Fans, Delight!

MIKE GREENBERG

NEW YORK TIMES BESTSELLING AUTHOR AND ESPN PERSONALITY

WITH PAUL "HEMBO" HEMBEKIDES

GOT YOUR NUMBER

THE GREATEST SPORTS LEGENDS AND THE NUMBERS THEY OWN

MIKE GREENBERG

NEW YORK TIMES BESTSELLING AUTHOR AND ESPN PERSONALITY

WITH PAUL "HEMBO" HEMBEKIDES

GOT YOUR ANSWERS

THE 100 GREATEST SPORTS ARGUMENTS—SETTLED

HYPERION AVENUE